WORKING FOR CANADA

To Kevin,

Hope you enjoy this book, that outlines a few more successes than any achieved by the beavers.

Best wishes,

Geoff McLub.

BEYOND BOUNDARIES: CANADIAN DEFENCE AND STRATEGIC STUDIES SERIES

Rob Huebert, Series Editor
ISSN 1716-2645 (Print) ISSN 1925-2919 (Online)

Canada's role in international military and strategic studies ranges from peacebuilding and Arctic sovereignty to unconventional warfare and domestic security. This series provides narratives and analyses of the Canadian military from both an historical and a contemporary perspective.

UNIVERSITY OF CALGARY
Press

WORKING FOR CANADA

A Pilgrimage in Foreign Affairs from the New World Order to the Rise of Populism

GEOFF WHITE

Beyond Boundaries:
Canadian Defence and Strategic Studies Series
ISSN 1716-2645 (Print) ISSN 1925-2919 (Online)

University of Calgary Press
2500 University Drive NW
Calgary, Alberta
Canada T2N 1N4
press.ucalgary.ca

LIBRARY AND ARCHIVES CANADA CATALOGUING IN PUBLICATION

Title: Working for Canada : a pilgrimage in foreign affairs from the New World Order to the rise of populism / Geoff White.
Names: White, Geoff (Author of Working for Canada), author.
Series: Beyond boundaries series ; no. 11.
Description: Series statement: Beyond boundaries : Canadian defence and strategic studies series, 1716-2645 ; no. 11 | Includes bibliographical references.
Identifiers: Canadiana (print) 20220388776 | Canadiana (ebook) 20220388946 | ISBN 9781773851938 (softcover) | ISBN 9781773851945 (open access PDF) | ISBN 9781773851952 (PDF) | ISBN 9781773851969 (EPUB)
Subjects: LCSH: White, Geoff (Author of Working for Canada) | LCSH: Canada. Global Affairs Canada—Officials and employees—Biography. | LCSH: Canada—Foreign relations. | LCGFT: Autobiographies.
Classification: LCC FC641.W55 A3 2022 | DDC 971.07092—dc23

The University of Calgary Press acknowledges the support of the Government of Alberta through the Alberta Media Fund for our publications. We acknowledge the financial support of the Government of Canada. We acknowledge the financial support of the Canada Council for the Arts for our publishing program.

Cover image: Colourbox 38717771
Cover design, page design, and typesetting by Melina Cusano

Contents

Prologue

Thirty years ago, on November 1, 1990, I joined the Government of Canada and – to be exact – the Department of External Affairs and International Trade, as Global Affairs Canada was then called. By sheer chance, the three ensuing decades of my career in international relations encompassed what is now evident as a distinct historical era in international affairs. We witnessed the astonishing end of the Cold War and the fall of communism, the arrival of the so-called "new world order," and the apparent triumph of liberal internationalism. More recently we have seen a surge in populist and authoritarian politics that seems to be changing the global rulebook on diplomacy and trade. When I retired in 2018, it was as though my career had ridden an arc from the hopeful beginning of a new era to its increasingly alarming end.

French memoirist François-René Chateaubriand, having lived through the final years of the French monarchy, the Revolution, and the Bourbon restoration, wrote: "I found myself between two centuries as at the junction of two rivers. I plunged into their troubled waters distancing myself with regret from the old shore where I was born, swimming with hope towards the unknown shore."[1] Chateaubriand's early life passed mostly in obscurity – as has my career in foreign affairs. Yet he wrote at the end of the 18th and beginning of the 19th centuries during a time of social and political transformations in some ways similar to those of our own era.

This book is offered with no view to exalt my modest role, working backstage in Canada's foreign and trade policy. But rather I want to offer some insight into what it's like to work within the organization now known as Global Affairs Canada; to cast some light on the nature of international policy work; and perhaps demystify some aspects of Canadian diplomacy.

Wordsworth's famous incantation – "Bliss it was in that dawn to be alive"[2]– could be applied to the days when the Berlin Wall was literally smashed down in 1989, heralding the end of the Cold War. In the following years, after I walked through the doors of External Affairs' Lester B. Pearson Building for the first time as an employee of the Government of Canada, my work would take me through a variety of assignments, all tied in one way or another to the broader international environment, as in the following highlights I try to show:

- The arrival of the "new world order," rather than ushering in a world where we would harvest the so-called peace dividend, brought surprising strife. My first assignment brought me into communications planning for the 1991 Persian Gulf War. It was a period of unexpected stress and fear.

- International economic liberalism held clear sway once the central planning model of the old Soviet bloc was discredited. More countries accepted the primacy of market forces and adhered to the multilateral trade regime under what would become the World Trade Organization. The North American Free Trade Agreement (NAFTA), for which I drafted and managed the communications strategy, was a major building block in this world-wide phenomenon of open markets and multilateral rules.

- The old east bloc was not smoothly integrated into Europe, despite the hopes of the time. The horrors of a genocidal war waged by Serbia against Bosnia helped germinate the "responsibility to protect" doctrine that underscored NATO's later intervention in Kosovo. Communications efforts to which I contributed during this conflict linked Canada's participation to our "human security agenda."

- Major progress in nuclear disarmament was a signal achievement following the easing of East-West tensions. Canada, through an initiative in the then-G8, was willing to do its part. Canada would play a role by offering to convert some of the uranium in Russian nuclear weapons to nuclear fuel in Canada. Trying to win the Canadian public's support for that undertaking – never fully achieved – proved to be a communications challenge.

- The new is always weighed down by the inertia of the past. The architecture of the world's system of aviation, establishing country-to-country negotiations of commercial airline routes, was hailed as a major international achievement under the Chicago Convention of 1949. More recent efforts to modernize this system met conservative resistance. I had the privilege to take part in the re-negotiation of many of these old-school, "mercantilist" agreements, as well as efforts to achieve more open skies.

- Despite the benefits of the NAFTA for the movement of virtually all goods between Canada, the United States and Mexico, trade in softwood lumber continued as a perennial sore point in bilateral Canada-US trade. I headed the softwood lumber controls division set up under the 2006 softwood lumber agreement, the fourth such arrangement in nearly three decades of arguing.

- Modern diplomatic methods under the rubric of "soft power" did not always have avid supporters when some political leaders gave priority to the more readily understood tangibles of economic growth and national security. Promoting abstractions such as Canada's international brand did not meet the favour of the Canadian government of the day. I was handed the controversial task of dismantling one of the programs in Foreign Affairs' "soft power" toolbox, the longstanding international arts promotion program (Promart).

- The dissolution of the racist, apartheid regime in South Africa was practically contemporary with the fall of communism. The remarkable struggle waged by South Africa's people to eventually found the "Rainbow Nation" was historic. I was accorded the great honour of serving in Canada's high commission (embassy) in South Africa. I witnessed the country's efforts to maintain its democracy and advance the wellbeing of its people. Yet misunderstandings and clashing attitudes toward various world developments strained the Canadian-South Africa friendship.

- In the island state of Madagascar, a Canadian mining company was leading the way in investment that could improve the economic prospects of that country's long-struggling economy. I had the responsibility to negotiate with the government terms that would allow the company to bring its investment to fruition. At the same time, I was involved in diplomatic efforts aimed at restoring the island's democracy.

- There were few better examples of the triumph of liberal democracy and the success of a market-oriented world view than the republic of Chile, even though the country still struggles with inequality and class resentment. I was the latest in a succession of senior trade commissioners who enjoyed promoting the prosperous trade and investment relationship between Canada and this remarkable country. The work of many Canadian firms demonstrated that "corporate social responsibility" was more than a marketing catch phrase. I later witnessed Chile's spearheading efforts to salvage the Trans- Pacific Partnership trade agreement after US President Donald Trump's withdrawal from the accord.

Shadows obscured the international stage as I took leave of Global Affairs in 2018 after nearly 30 years. The rise of American isolationism, growing authoritarianism worldwide – whether in China, Russia, Hungary or Brazil – did indeed suggest one era was ending and another was struggling to begin.

The German philosopher Georg Friedrich Hegel invoked an ancient Greek legend as a metaphor for the transformation of the historical order. "The owl of Minerva spreads its wings only at the coming of dusk . . . We are . . . agents in a drama we do not really understand. Only after we have played it out do we understand what has been afoot all the time"[3] Is the curtain now opening on an era for which we have not prepared ourselves, replete with new challenges only dimly illuminated?

When I joined the government, like all federal civil servants, I swore the following oath. "I will faithfully and honourably fulfil the duties that devolve on me by reason of my employment in the public service of Canada and I will not, without due authority, disclose or make known any matter that comes to my knowledge by reason of such employment." As has been made clear on several occasions in legal proceedings, this oath must always be read in the context of Canadians' right to freedom of expression.

The loyalty oath exists in parallel with two important pieces of federal legislation: the Access to Information Act, in which the public has a right to information, subject only to defined exemptions, and the Security of Information Act, a successor of the Official Secrets Act, which among other things, prohibits the disclosure of special operational information. Conscious of all of the above, I have shared a manuscript of this book with Global Affairs Canada before publication. I believe this book is informed by my loyalty as a long-serving civil servant, now retired.

Global Affairs Canada has the essential mission of protecting Canada's security and promoting the country's prosperity. It would have been my great honour and privilege to have worked for this institution – and for Canada – at any time, but especially so during a remarkably fascinating era. Any criticism that may be inferred from the following pages is not intended to disparage the important work of the Department. But diplomacy and government processes have their flaws which often need to be aired and reflected upon.

My hope is that, in reading this book, Canadians interested in our foreign and trade policy, and especially those who may be interested in a career in international affairs, will have a somewhat better insight as to how, at a practical level, Canadian diplomacy works.

This book spans a range of issues pertinent to the period but is by no means comprehensive in scope. Other Global Affairs employees would give quite different accounts. Their narratives would involve other issues, and they would express their own perspectives. Nevertheless, my assignments were certainly broadly representative of the Department's work during nearly three decades, and probably covered a wider variety of issues and themes than most employees had the privilege to be exposed to. My previous career as a journalist who covered a wide variety of subjects perhaps gave the Department's management the confidence to entrust me with the spectrum of files that I managed over those years.

What follows is an account of my pilgrimage through an historical landscape initially characterized by an optimism for a more just and prosperous world, but which, in the final stages, became dangerously contorted and beset with danger. The path to a renewed faith in international cohesion and trust will be arduous and demanding – as arduous and demanding as effective diplomacy itself. Devoted to a belief that a better international environment can be achieved, Canadian diplomacy will continue to offer the kind of opportunities and challenges that I, with many talented colleagues, took on during a nearly three-decade career working for Canada.

1

Breaking the Spell (1990–1991)

It was a sunny morning in upstate Vermont in August 1990 when I walked into the hotel dining room for a leisurely breakfast. I took the complimentary copy of *USA Today* from the concierge's desk and looked at the above-the-fold headline announcing that Iraqi armed forces had invaded Kuwait. It was a surprise attack, not rumoured in advance in any source that I was familiar with. I knew immediately that the job I had recently accepted at the Canadian Department of External Affairs and International Trade (as today's Global Affairs Canada was then known) would present an unanticipated challenge. It was pulse-quickening if not quite alarming.

My several-day sojourn in Vermont was part of a relaxed summer holiday. I had decided to leave my employer of 13 years, *The Calgary Herald*, as well as the profession of journalism, lured by a job at External Affairs, where I was to take on a role in so-called strategic communications.

The first half of 1990 had been intense. As the *Herald*'s Ottawa editor, I had covered the negotiations of the Meech Lake Accord, the amendment that was supposed to win Quebec's adherence to the Canadian Constitution. Talks that had begun in 1987 culminated in June 1990 at the Ottawa Conference Centre during virtually around-the-clock sessions between Prime Minister Brian Mulroney and the provincial premiers. It had been a tiring time, leading to a depressing aftermath. For all the effort that had been put into Meech Lake, the negotiations failed, and as ambivalent as I had been about the prospective result, I felt a sense of futility that so much energy had been expended on this empty outcome.

I had sometimes thought of changing my career. As a journalist, one is an observer of events, not a participant in them. A desire to play a more active role in public matters often draws reporters across the line to government, businesses or associations. There is even the wish sometimes of using experience on "the other side" to become a better journalist by plumbing the inner workings of the major organizations that make the news. So, I was pleased when, making a preliminary enquiry at External Affairs, I received a reply that the department would be interested in hiring me in their strategic communications division. I accepted an offer to start on November 1, 1990.

In Vermont then, I was taking advantage of the opportunity to ease out of one career into another. Once I joined the Department, I expected the adjustment to be stressful, but I also expected the opportunity to tackle my new role in a methodical fashion, learning the ropes in an atmosphere not too intensely agitated by an aura of crisis. Once I read the headline in *USA Today*, I suspected that the Department would be confronting something it hadn't had to in many years.

It is impossible to overstate the change in the international landscape at the start of the final decade of the 20th century. Conventional belief held that the Cold War, the strategic framework on which international relations had been built since the late '40s, was an almost permanent state, to prevail long into the next century. The communist domination of the Soviet Union and Eastern Europe was apparently intractable. Virtually no one envisaged changes coming from within the east bloc. If these were to come, they would be evolutionary and slow. For some thinkers, a dissolution of dictatorship could be coaxed into being by a careful dialogue between Communist capitals and European liberal and social democratic governments. This would ease the tight-wound coils of suspicion, open the East to experimenting with market reforms and encourage a "convergence" between the two world systems. Instead, the rapid collapse of communism from 1987 to 1993 was a stunning turn of events of really unbelievable magnitude.

History was undoubtedly turning a page. The Cold War, characterized by geopolitical inertia and ideological bondage, was being given its last rites. But we didn't know what the next chapter would hold. We would learn that Saddam Hussein's 1990 invasion of Iraq was one of the opening sallies in a quite different historical phase in which a predominant theme was the rise of Islamic fundamentalism and its confrontation with the liberty of the secular world.

On November 1, 1990, I walked from downtown Ottawa along Sussex Drive to the Lester B. Pearson Building, since 1973 the headquarters of the Department of External Affairs and International Trade (today known as Global Affairs Canada). My coat was tightly belted and buttoned against the truly seasonal northeast wind, and the walk seemed longer than I expected. The grey and blustery day wasn't conducive to a new beginning. I entered through the heavy metal doors of in the principal entrance and turned left from the foyer towards the "D tower."

The Pearson Building is a sprawling structure that is said to have been designed to resemble the Sphinx, in abstract obeisance to Prime Minister Lester Pearson's peacekeeping role in the Middle East during the Suez crisis. Its main A tower represents the Sphinx's imposing head and the C and D towers its powerful paws, all aligned in a northerly direction evoking Canada's role as a northern power. To me, the building looks more like a ship's bridge, evoking the command centre of Canada's ship of state. I am always reminded of Leonard Cohen's rare optimistic anthem: "Sail on, sail on, O mighty ship of state, To the shores of need, Past the reefs of Greed, Through the Squalls of Hate."[1]

In the D tower was housed all the department's administrative functions, including human resources. In one of the partitioned cubicles, I located my staffing officer, Luc Cousineau, who then found the papers that I needed to sign, including the rather sweeping Loyalty Oath.[2]

"Have you had any previous government experience?" Cousineau asked. "No," I said. "Too bad," he replied. "For pension purposes, you could 'buy back' those years and get out of here a lot sooner." Hardly a happy welcome to a radiant future in the elysian fields of Canadian foreign and trade policy.

The man most responsible for my hiring was Peter Daniel, who was then the assistant deputy minister of communications and culture. The bland title, assistant deputy minister, or ADM does not evoke to government outsiders the force and weight it carries within the federal bureaucracy. Whereas deputy ministers are the top civil servants of any department and are in regular though rarefied contact with the elected ministers, ADMs wield real and effective day-to-day authority over sprawling departmental branches. They give the overall direction and are, more often than not, the arbiters of even pedestrian decisions in their domains. Daniel was a rarity within the federal civil service structure. Only at Finance Canada and External Affairs at that time were there ADMs responsible for communications branches. Elsewhere, running communications, which entailed explaining departments' policies and actions to a variety of audiences – media, business, associations, employees or the general public – was subsumed within other administrative streams – likely a policy or functional branch. That the communications function was accorded its own branch at External was an indicator of the importance ascribed to it in managing foreign and trade policy.

Daniel was himself a former journalist, having worked for the Canadian Broadcasting Corporation in Montreal. Even today, whenever there are documentaries that recall the 1970 October Crisis, one inevitably sees footage of a young and handsome Daniel announcing to viewers the discovery of Quebec Labour Minister Pierre Laporte's body in the trunk of a car following the minister's assassination by militants of a cell of the Front de Libération du Québec. I had met Daniel on numerous occasions at networking functions hosted by the Department – either policy events or visits of heads of state or foreign ministers. He seemed to be sufficiently impressed with my journalistic credentials and demeanour to consider me a prospect for his branch. Daniel was not, in 1990, quite the photogenic TV broadcaster of 20 years before. With his carefully managed comb-over and pale skin, and his habit of draping his overcoat across his shoulders, he had acquired the nickname "the Count," which reflected an attitude of some affection but also a little fear in those who reported to him. Daniel would hold court from behind a specially designed circular desk in his office on the second floor of the "C tower" which overlooked Ottawa's old City Hall by the final reaches of the Rideau River. It was there that I was first informed of my initial assignment in the Department: to work as a strategist on trade communications. I was to be involved in explaining and promoting a variety of trade initiatives, including trade agreements, handling questions regarding international trade disputes, and devising and managing publicity campaigns for Canada's Trade Commissioner Service. But Saddam Hussein's invasion of Kuwait changed that. Rather than supporting the economic interests of a country at peace, I would be recruited into the civil service rear-guard of a highly unexpected military campaign.

The role Canada would play in the wake of the invasion of Kuwait was not immediately obvious. The attack was a clear violation of Kuwait's national sovereignty. There had not been, since Vietnam's invasion of Cambodia during the unsettled period following the United States' 1975 withdrawal from Vietnam, such an indisputable and complete flouting of the territorial integrity of a United Nations member country. Iraq's motive was to seize Kuwait's petroleum resources, giving it greater control over future supply of oil to international markets. The Iraqi Army's presence in Kuwait was made more forbidding by the positioning of its troops along the Saudi Arabian border, opening the possibility of another armed confrontation that could have a significant impact on world petroleum supplies. Yes, memories of world oil shortages familiar from Middle East conflicts in the '70s were on everyone's minds. But international condemnation focussed on the principle of preservation of national sovereignty within internationally recognized borders.

Almost universally negative reaction to the invasion led to the rare unanimous resolution of the United Nations Security Council to call for the use of "all necessary powers" to dislodge Saddam from Kuwait. With the support of this resolution, United States President George H. W. Bush (the first Bush, not the second) announced that the United States would assemble a coalition of like-minded countries to restore Kuwait's sovereignty.

Canada's reputation was linked to our "traditional" peacekeeping role, and that suggested it was unlikely that Canada would play a direct military role in repelling the invasion. But the government of Prime Minister Mulroney, which was more inclined to align itself closely with the United States than any of its Liberal predecessors, was in fact prepared to play a more active part. Prime Minister Mulroney committed to President Bush that Canada would contribute militarily to an effort to dislodge Saddam from Kuwait on the condition that action be mandated by the United Nations. Mulroney thereby opened the door to Canada's taking part in a war for the first time since the Korean War 40 years before.

The tension about this significant shift in Canada's policy is captured in Mulroney's speech to the House of Commons: "The Commons was tense as I got to my feet on January 15th. As I began my remarks, protestors in the galleries began chanting, "No war. No war." With Canadian lives on the line, I understood and respected the emotion behind the voices shouting at me. If [Saddam] Hussein acted the way I suspected he would [by not respecting the January 15th, 1991 deadline to withdraw from Kuwait] I knew in a few short days I would become the first prime minister since Louis St-Laurent to commit Canadian soldiers, airmen, and sailors to battle. Hussein had made clear his threats to use weapons of mass destruction against coalition troops, making my government's decision all the more chilling. 'The question before Canadians now is a simple one,' I told the House. 'If Saddam Hussein does not withdraw peacefully from Kuwait and the use of force is required, where will Canada stand? On this simple question of right and wrong, will we continue to support the international coalition, or will we stand aside and hope that others will uphold the rule of international law?"[3]

When within days of my joining the Department, the approximately 200 employees of the communications and culture branch were assembled in the Department's formal conference room to learn of their new assignment, the atmosphere was tense. I and many others in the room that day were of the generation that had watched and sympathized with the ordeal of the United States and Vietnam and its neighbours during the American war in Indochina. The United States' defeat in 1975; the deaths of so many young American soldiers; the destruction and death unleashed on the Vietnamese; the flight of Vietnamese "boat people" following the conflict. Although Canada had played little official role in these events, other than as a member of the rather toothless international control commissions that supervised brief truces near the beginning and the end of the war, the conflict had a major impact on my generation. From the perspective of many of us, having seen the impact of this conflict, advocacy of armed force to solve world crises was almost unspeakable. After its defeat in Vietnam, the chastened United States was reluctant to put US soldiers in harm's way in a foreign conflict. And Canadians sympathized.

Daniel made it clear that – using an expression from the First World War referring to warning of an impending attack – "when the balloon went up," we must all be prepared to endure difficult moments. As I would learn throughout my employment with the Department, government priorities usually demand the participation of employees from well outside their nominally defined roles. Daniel wanted commitment from across his whole branch. We were to run an around-the-clock media monitoring and analysis operation which would advise the privy council, cabinet and ultimately the prime minister. We were to cover rapidly evolving international developments; outline the manner in which these were being characterized; and propose "messages" to assist ministers explaining Canada's position to the public. We would be organized in three rotating shifts in an expanded departmental operations centre. We would often be reporting for work at midnight and relinquishing our shifts at 8 am. Daniel announced that, should there be those who objected to Canada's military participation in the Gulf War, their views would be respected, and they would continue in their regular jobs – although with added tasks given their colleagues' absence on the Gulf communications team.

Never for a moment did I consider not taking part. My opposition to the Vietnam War was well known during my university years, but I had never espoused pacifism. To me the clear violation of Kuwait's sovereignty was something that could not be ignored and thereby condoned. Acquiescing to this invasion would embolden others and threaten peace elsewhere. But I respected the decision of some of my new colleagues to stand down.

The team began work at the beginning of January 1991. Our location was a narrow office alongside the Department's 24-hour operations centre. It was immediately adjacent to the "crisis" situation room where senior officials from the various government departments involved assembled early each morning to review intelligence and coordinate next actions. The office was equipped with terminals providing access to national and international wire services, as well as television monitors that were invariably tuned to CNN, which at that time had just passed its first decade of operation. The internet was in its infancy and known only to a handful of specialist government and academic institutions. There was no Twitter, no Facebook. Email at the time was rudimentary and patchy within the federal government, and was not the core office mode of communication it has since become. I was the designated analyst for whichever shift I was on, and it was my role to monitor all relevant media, oversee the production of a media summary to highlight new and pertinent information and then provide an analysis for the policy coordinating committee. The most important scan and analysis was the one produced for the daily

7 am meeting. This piece would be combined with analyses from the Privy Council Office (effectively the top executive suite of the Canadian federal public service), an "issues summary" from the Department of National Defence (DND) and a domestic media survey from a Toronto-based team headed by University of Toronto professor John Kirton. Based on these inputs the crisis communications committee would adjust the government's daily messaging. The principal message to which the government must adhere, according to the communications strategy devised in the run-up to the creation of the task force, was that every action undertaken by the government was consistent with the United Nations-approved mandate under Security Council Resolution 278.[4]

A new recruit to the Department, I was now being exposed to its complex processes and internal machinations, including those around the production of any statement designed for media consumption. Each shift would have a media relations officer to field reporters' questions. If there was no previously approved response to a query, it was the team's responsibility to produce one. But only after the proposed response had been vetted by the appropriate geographic or policy branch. This was far from the freewheeling climate of a news bureau that I was used to, where you expected what you wrote to appear in print, perhaps only lightly touched by a copyeditor. I remember a rather uncomfortable exchange with the manager of the Department's operations centre. Reviewing a few rather anodyne lines to answer a fairly simple media question, he shouted red-facedly: "Has Chuck Svoboda seen this? He must approve it before it goes out!" Svoboda, director, as I recall it, of international security, in the mystified tone of someone who was wondering why he was being bothered, gave the lines his weary go-ahead. But I had to get used to the often draining and turgid process of approvals and re-writes and re-approvals that often had to work their way upward through the hierarchy even to ministers' offices.

The evening of January 16th, 1991 was unforgettable. Saddam Hussein had been presented with an ultimatum to withdraw his troops from Iraq on January 15. That deadline having passed without any response, President Bush announced that the assault against Iraq would begin, which initially would involve the bombardment of Iraqi military positions and installations, including in the capital Baghdad.

What we saw on live television was a revelation. First, live images of the night sky above Baghdad illuminated by tracer lights attempting to reveal incoming US cruise missiles. Then, broadcast coverage directly from US aircraft identifying ground targets and displaying the hits made by the cruise missiles, broadcast from the on-screen computer terminals in the cockpits of the aircraft. Such imagery is considered routine today, but this was the first time any of this technology had been used in wartime and the first time such images had been broadcast live to an international television audience. My colleagues and I, as did television audiences everywhere, watched in amazement as the air assault unfolded before our eyes.

This was the first of many such nights during the opening attacks of the Gulf War. As night after night of air sorties against Iraq ground on, we began to think the war could be a protracted one. If the barrage of bombings was taking weeks, would the ground campaign which would follow against Saddam Hussein's supposedly highly trained, elite troops known as the Republican Guard not take even longer? And wouldn't a ground war bring allied coalition casualties that the air war was largely immune to? The mood among the communications team was resigned and anxious.

Each media analysis was drafted in an atmosphere of dread. This war could have decidedly bloody consequences that would include terrible casualties for all sides, including Canadian military personnel. There was never, however, any event that caused any notable deviation from the communications team's "main messages" relating to Canada's steadfast support for a United Nations-approved military intervention. As the war ground on the "principal themes" outlined in the evolving 48-hour communication plan were: "Recognition and empathy for the human, economic and environmental costs of war; responsible management of the Canadian war effort; [and] the need to keep our values intact – domestic tolerance; honouring international obligations; protecting international peace and order."[5]

Our objective was to advance and give credence to the government's stance. But the specific role of our forces evolved from the moment their deployment was announced. Three battleships in the Persian Gulf were to enforce a United Nations-imposed embargo on Iraqi trade. But then their role was expanded to provide protection to other allied forces in the Gulf.

A squadron of CF-18 fighter jets were to patrol the skies above the Gulf to identify any Iraqi aircraft posing a threat to Coalition aircraft participating in the bombardment. But, as will be seen, that role escalated to a more aggressive posture.

The constantly shifting war aims were not an ideal basis for communications management. In the best of situations, communications are carefully planned in advance under a pre-determined scenario. But in this case, the government was adjusting its posture as preparations to confront Saddam evolved. Our role, rather than explaining our actions within a defined strategy, was to help bring public sentiment along as war aims broadened. The challenge was to convince audiences that the government, in constantly adjusting its stance, was exercising good judgment within a framework of accepted Canadian values.

Canadian public opinion had been initially supportive of military action and of possible Canadian involvement. In September 1990, an Angus Reid poll found that 69 per cent of Canadians favoured the government's decision to send forces to the Gulf in support of sanctions. However, by mid-January, with military action directly involving Canadian troops seeming much more likely, support had slipped to 36 per cent.[6]

In our stance, we were moving from a peacekeeping paradigm to one of active aggression. The attention brought to bear on "the first shot" taken by the Canadian military reflected our critical awareness of Canada's new stance. At the outset of the aerial bombardment of Iraq, Canadian fighter jets did not take part. Instead, they were to intercept any Iraqi aircraft attacking coalition fighters and bombers, including those in hot pursuit of allied bombers returning from their nightly missions. However, on the night of January 30, two Canadian airmen were ordered, as they were the best positioned in the Gulf skies, to attack an Iraqi missile-carrying ship seeking refuge in an Iranian port. They pursued and severely damaged the vessel and were then thrust into the limelight as the first Canadian warriors since the Korean War to have attacked – not in a defensive, but in an aggressive, posture – enemy forces.[7]

Canadian media duly reported this incident although it was a mosquito's bite compared to the massive nightly wolf pack attacks of US fighter-bombers on targets throughout Iraq. Yet the incident effectively broke the spell under which, for more than 35 years, Canada and the Canadian public had been bound. We had been proud of our reputation as non-aggressors and peacekeepers. We had not during those many years taken any direct military action against any other state. Crossing that Rubicon was profoundly significant. The event raised concerns even in DND headquarters where "Colonel Richard Bastien said that the attack may have been technically beyond the authorized role in the Persian Gulf, but it was within the spirit of the rules of Canadian engagement."[8] So it was illustrative of the *post facto* communications approach that, only after the CF-18 assault on the Iraqi vessel, did Defence Minister Bill McKnight announce that the fleet of CF-18s would henceforth be permitted to launch direct attacks against Iraqi forces.

Discomfort over our newfound belligerence erupted behind-the-scenes on the eve of the much-anticipated ground assault when it appeared that a Soviet-brokered deal could avert the oncoming battle. Scrawled in hand on the National Library-archived version of the daily Gulf communications report was the following: "Only one story [today]. Iraq ready to talk. [Convening of] Arab summit, redistribution of wealth, and elimination of weapons of mass destruction [all elements of the Soviet-Iraqi proposal] . . . That is along the line of the Canadian government post-hostilities proposal."

I do not know who the author of the annotation was, although it would have been a senior official either in External Affairs or the Privy Council. But it was evident that he or she was desperate for a lifeline to peace and a halt to the momentum of the war machine. At the highest level of our Gulf crisis planning, there was the hope that the conflict could be ended without a land campaign. My own analysis of the prospective Soviet-brokered deal in an analysis drafted for the 7 am task force meeting was that failing to take advantage of it could be a source of future recriminations. "The outcome and intensity of this debate will be affected by the success [or failure] of the ground battle. If the war goes well, the argument [over a possible lost opportunity for a peace deal] will become marginal. If it goes poorly, it will become a major source of controversy."

It is a civil servant's job to advise. It is ministers' jobs to dispose. My words of caution appeared to gain no traction. Evident jitters among senior officials didn't change the government's course. The official line devised in response to the Soviet plan was that it fell short. It did not include

Iraq's immediate disavowal of heavy weaponry; nor its accepted responsibility for paying war reparations; nor renunciation of its territorial claim to Kuwait. Holding back the drumbeat for war was not to be countenanced at this late stage. A Canadian diplomat who had been evacuated from Kuwait observed: "The only language Saddam Hussein is capable of understanding is that of violence, and there is no possibility of peace while he is in power."[9]

With the ground attack about to begin, there was terrible foreboding about the carnage that might follow. On February 23, the United States and other coalition forces crossed into Kuwait and Iraq from bases in Saudi Arabia. Within a few hours, media were reporting the surrender and capture of the supposedly fearsome Iraqi forces who had been panicked into surrender and flight. President Bush would announce on February 27 that Kuwait had been freed and the Iraqi armed forces defeated.

A war in the Persian Gulf was hardly what was envisioned by anyone as the opening chapter of the post-Cold War era. The collapse of communism in the Soviet Union and eastern Europe was to have brought a "peace dividend" of closer international cooperation and an era of peace. Perhaps the Soviet Union's efforts under Mikhail Gorbachev to mediate a solution predicated on Iraq's withdrawal from Kuwait appeared closer to embodying the possibilities of "the new world order." But by the time that initiative was broached, the United States and its allies, including Canada, were already committed to bringing Saddam Hussein to heel by military force.

Today the 1991 Persian Gulf War must be seen as the opening act of an era of wars, intra-state conflict and terrorism. For Canada, it foreshadowed the first of several military actions, including in Kosovo and Afghanistan, where the decisions to take part were made easier by the Persian Gulf precedent.

For the External Affairs communications team, the end of the war was a great relief. I vividly remember being told on March 1 that the group was being disbanded and we would return to our normal departmental roles. I was on the day shift when the news came, and I walked directly from the operations centre to the offices of the communications bureau. The sun was shining. Spring seemed to be in the air. But moments after arriving in the office, I heard a series of muffled explosions that shook the

Pearson Building's foundation. Surely it wasn't possible? Had opposition to Canada's role in the war taken a violent turn? Was this the act of saboteurs aggrieved at the defeat of an Arab nation by US imperialism?

I hardly had time to ask. My colleagues smiled, unperturbed. The explosions were part of the routine, annual campaign to break up the ice on the Rideau River. The blasts were needed to stop ice jams flooding the New Edinburgh neighbourhood on the opposite shore. My brief panic passed.

I felt easier than I had since the previous summer. I was finally about to begin my "peacetime" duties in the Department. The end of the war was a relief. There was some belief that successfully restraining Iraq was proof that regional conflicts could be contained and that the post-Cold War era would continue to yield benefits for global peace and stability.

As Foreign Affairs Minister Joe Clark said to the Standing Committee on External Affairs and International Trade in the wake of the war on March 21: "The next six months, at most the next year, will be critical for determining whether the war with Iraq will go down in history as the key which opened a whole new era in the Middle East."

Well, it *was* a key that opened a whole new era in the Middle East, but not in the way Clark was hoping. We would eventually witness the attack on the World Trade Centre on September 11, 2001; the long war in Afghanistan to supplant Al Qaeda and the Taliban; the more violent and destabilizing second act of the war on Iraq in 2003; and the eruption of the Islamic State in Iraq and Syria. These were not direct consequences of the Persian Gulf War; but the war was a precursor for dark, new forces to be unleashed in the world.

In this new period, traditional peacekeeping, for which Canada had been renowned, has been called upon less and less to intervene in armed disputes. In joining the Persian Gulf allied coalition, Canada was crossing the threshold into a different era which would make us define in some new way our stance toward international conflict.

It has been said that peacekeeping can be applied where there is a peace to keep, usually between warring states. That implies that the states – even reluctantly – recognize the benefit of being kept apart. The conflicts of the last three post-Cold War decades seem not to have provided such grounds for mutual restraint. Rather they have often been characterized by the will of a state or non-state actor to impose its will on vulnerable populations and brook no efforts at mediation. There is "a gap between the traditional principles of peacekeeping – impartiality, consent of the parties, and the use of force only in self-defence or to protect civilians – and . . . moving towards peace enforcement and counter-terrorism."[10] The Canadian participation in the United Nations' Multidimensional Integrative Stabilization Mission to Mali (MINUSMA) was a case in point. Canada's involvement ended in September 2019. But its purpose was to provide military support to protect the local population against the aggression of unrepentant Islamic jihadists who did not and still will not talk peace.

In 1990, it was an unexpected experience to witness at first-hand how the Canadian government strained to adjust to new circumstances with the outbreak of the Persian Gulf War. But back on regular duty in the communications branch, where I was to devise communications strategy in support of Canadian trade policy, I had the start of my next assignment to ponder. Little noticed by me during the last two months in the Gulf communications task force was the announcement by International Trade Minister John Crosbie on February 5, 1991, that Canada was about to join negotiations for a free trade agreement with the United States and Mexico.

Explaining NAFTA (1991–1993)

My *Calgary Herald* colleague Peter Morton and I were treating ourselves to a steak at Hy's, in the late '80s Ottawa powerbrokers' "lunchroom," when I noticed we were seated beside Simon Reisman, former deputy minister of finance and later chief negotiator of the Canada-United States Free Trade Agreement (FTA). I could hear snatches of conversation between him and his lunch companion which touched on interpretations of some passages of the Torah. It was a gentle exchange on an obscure topic for me, and quite at odds with Reisman's well-known aggressive manner. Reisman had the physical presence of a British bulldog, and this civil exchange with someone who was evidently a family friend revealed another facet of one of Ottawa's most powerful civil servants.

This was not the side of the man I knew. Most memorably in the fall of 1987, I was the target of a more characteristically pugnacious Reisman sally during a news conference to release the highlights of the just-negotiated FTA. Just negotiated, I say. Several days had followed the conclusion of the talks at midnight on October 4 leaving a vacuum for speculation about what the agreement actually contained.

At long last, a news conference was called on October 8 in the Government Conference Centre where Reisman spoke to a thin "elements of the deal" document which outlined the agreement's key measures. What caught my attention was the energy provision that guaranteed that the United States would receive – during any rationing of energy due to future market shortages – the same proportion of energy supply accorded Canadians. That is, Canada would not be allowed to reduce sales to the US market to protect supply for Canadian domestic needs.

The news conference was packed. The press corps filled most of the available seats in the room, which at one time served as the main lobby of the Ottawa train station and is today the temporary home of the Canadian Senate. Reisman was installed on the long dais at the end of the hall flanked by other federal officials. I considered myself lucky to be recognized to ask a question, and I immediately drew attention to what appeared at first glance to be a ceding of Canadian sovereignty over energy resources. Reisman's response was forceful, dismissive and derisory. "It's just boiler-plate," he declaimed. Nothing more than what Canada is obliged to do under the International Energy Agency (IEA) agreement, one of numerous multilateral conventions. I didn't buy it, but his assertions had to be checked, which delay would further impede public understanding of the FTA. After months of lengthy negotiations and several days after the deal's official announcement, the surprise disclosure of the unanticipated energy chapter represented a terrible lapse in government communications, and it became one of the major targets of the simmering opposition to the free trade deal.[1]

I had this incident very much in mind, when Peter Daniel called me to his office to tell me that he was putting me in charge of developing and implementing the communications plan for the negotiation of the North American Free Trade Agreement (NAFTA). In responding to Peter, I emphasized that in, my opinion, the communications of the FTA had been badly fumbled. Much of the suspicion that had arisen about the deal stemmed from the mystery that had surrounded the details after its announcement. As was later described in a history of the FTA talks by three of its participants: "The period from October 4 to December 11 [when the text was published] . . . took on a surreal quality . . . Deadlines came and went. Days became night and weekends evaporated into the following week . . . The drama was played out against the background of an increasingly sceptical audience, while the battle for the hearts and minds of Canadians appeared to be going to the opposition. The delay in producing the final text did not help the cause."[2] In the understandable absence of a definitive final text, the agreement would have been better received had a complete description of its provisions been released upon signature. I was impressed when Daniel agreed with me and said that we would seek to accomplish just that with the NAFTA, should negotiations succeed. And from that moment at the beginning of March in 1991 until the successful conclusion of the talks in August 1992, my team and I worked to achieve that very concrete and feasible objective.

It was April before the government's chief negotiator was announced. John Weekes, who was brought on board after serving several years as Canada's ambassador to the GATT (General Agreement on Tariffs and Trade, the precursor to the World Trade Organization), could hardly have been more different than Reisman. He was gentlemanly and collegial, and in a career almost entirely taken up with trade policy assignments, was perhaps Canada's foremost expert and practitioner in the field. The way Weekes was to structure the NAFTA negotiations office reflected the specialized – and, to many, arcane – features of the trade policy craft. In addition to specialists on "market access," in which tariff reductions and elimination were the goal, there were also experts on trade remedies, dispute resolution, investment and services. There were other experts, some recruited from the departments of industry and agriculture, on specific sectors such as autos, textiles and clothing, and agricultural products. The NAFTA team was a large interdepartmental organization recruiting a substantial pool of talent that befit an enterprise charged with no less than negotiating the trade rules for three economies comprising more than 350 million people. What was significant for me was that Daniel had prevailed in preserving independence for the communications function within the overall structure. Daniel guarded for his branch all responsibility for drafting the communications strategy and conferred directly with Weekes as an equal. As competent as trade policy mandarins are in their field, communications could have become a hostage to an overweening obsession with fine details that would make the public affairs program less manageable.

The NAFTA communications office was not huge. The group, which was responsible for liaising with the trade specialists, articulating the strategy and generating the content, represented no more than five people, although we called constantly on the general services offered by the trade and corporate communications services divisions.[3] I didn't know it at first, but the three years of negotiations that would last ultimately until January 1994 would become a period of almost interminable days of near-monastic dedication. I had never worked such long hours before, nor have I since. Our tiny suite of offices sandwiched in a second storey corner of the

C tower from which we could only see, over a gravelled roof, other offices in the B and D towers, contributed to the cloistered atmosphere. On the north side of the Pearson complex, our offices were in shadow for most of the year. Only during the summer months did a thin ray of sunshine between 1 and 3 pm penetrate the gloom.

The lack of receptivity of Canadians to the NAFTA was hardly encouraging. The original FTA had only been formally in place since 1989 and although some positive results of that deal were beginning to appear, the overall attitude of the Canadian public was deeply negative. Starting in the second quarter of 1990, the Canadian economy had fallen into a recession, and according to a March Angus Reid poll commissioned by External Affairs to help guide our communications strategy, 62 per cent of respondents blamed the FTA. By August 1991, Canadians' confidence in the government to guide the economy had sunk to 35 per cent. Some 72 per cent believed they had been personally hurt by the FTA. Curiously 46 per cent supported the negotiations for the NAFTA, but that relatively high level of support did not last long. By March 1992, it would sink to 29 per cent. The opposition of the public was characterized by the attitude: "If the FTA is bad, the NAFTA can only be worse."

Why was the government then pursuing this initiative? In the early '90s the conviction that globalization was inevitable and that all governments must seek to harvest its benefits was prevailing economic wisdom, sweeping up governments in all bands of the spectrum, right, centre and left. But opposition was vocal and vehement and would grow over time, led particularly by an array of "civil society" organizations, which not long after would so disrupt WTO negotiations in Seattle, Washington in 1999 that negotiators would literally flee the bargaining tables. Nonetheless, the mainstream consensus was that governments should facilitate the benefits of an increasingly global economy by striking down trade barriers while acting, if necessary, to mitigate negative impacts on previously protected, inefficient industries. This was certainly the underlying inspiration for the NAFTA and all subsequent trade agreements Canada pursued.

The NAFTA had its own particularities. The negotiations as first conceived by the United States were to have aimed at a bilateral deal only between the US and Mexico, and the Canadian government had become alarmed that preferential access by Mexico to the US market could undermine the hard-won gains of the original Canada-US FTA. Canada, therefore, proposed that we be included in a trilateral arrangement. After some initial pushback, particularly from the US, Mexico and Washington consented. A factor in President Bush's agreement was the warm relationship he had with Prime Minister Mulroney over the latter's efforts to rally international support for the UN-sanctioned Persian Gulf War. But there was a further important factor.

Both Canada and the United States saw a trade agreement with Mexico from the perspective of geopolitical security. A more developed, more prosperous Mexico would make the North American continent more secure, and less prone to poverty-induced problems of crime, illegal migration, and even political instability.

This theme formed part of the lengthy and detailed communications plan that I was asked to draft. After extensive consultation with the office of Trade and Industry Minister Michael Wilson as well as the civil service negotiators in what was called the Office of Trilateral Trade Negotiations (OTTN), the plan was presented and approved by cabinet along with the NAFTA negotiating mandate. In addition to calling for a detailed package of negotiating results once a deal was struck, the communications plan also recommended an ongoing series of public briefings on the issues at stake.

That perhaps-too-optimistic commitment to public outreach faltered in the early going. Part of the resistance came from Canada's ambassador to Washington, Derek Burney, who had been Prime Minister Mulroney's chief of staff and one of the key architects of the original FTA. In a diplomatic cable sent to the Department on June 5th, 1991 Burney said: "I am troubled by the high profile we seem to be giving NAFTA negotiations in Canada . . . Our primary objective in transforming the United States – Mexico negotiation into a trilateral negotiation was, and is, defensive – essentially to ensure that Canadian exports and Canadian attractiveness as an investment location are not damaged by US preferential treatment granted to Mexico or by emergence of different rules for trade and investment."[4] External's assistant deputy minister for United States relations before the start of the FTA negotiations, Burney generally subscribed to a foreign policy "realism" that put the United States wholly in the centre of Canadian foreign policy

The pre-eminence of Canada-US relations in Canada's foreign policy ought to be obvious, but it's an orientation that can smother other perspectives. And in this instance, the relative advantages of improving Canada's wider trade and foreign policy interests gave way to a preference for a much lower profile in a defensive posture. Burney was extremely critical of holding the kick-off negotiations in Toronto and advised against giving the talks too much momentum pending US elections in November 1992.

Burney's was not the only voice counselling caution about overselling the NAFTA. Michael Wilson, who had left the ministry of finance to become a kind of "super" minister responsible for both Industry Canada and International Trade, seeing the negative public attitudes about the government's economic management during the ongoing recession, thought that pitching the NAFTA as only one element in the new "Prosperity Agenda" would have the benefit of deflecting attention from the NAFTA talks. (The "Prosperity Agenda", like so many grandly labelled undertakings built more on rhetoric than actual programs, was difficult to pin down and would eventually evaporate towards the end of the government's electoral term). Other initiatives within the NAFTA negotiating mandate, to introduce for instance an accession clause that would allow other countries – such as Chile in particular – to join the NAFTA, lost momentum as the talks shifted toward the defensive, low profile stance that Burney and other realists advised.

That said, our NAFTA communications team with Daniel's support remained committed to the goal of ensuring a full and detailed communications package the instant the talks were concluded. The critical path for our project became clear after talks were held in Zacatecas, Mexico from October 26 to 27, 1991.

Keeping a low profile was not necessarily in the domestic interest of the Mexicans. While abiding by an agreement not to reveal important details of still-ongoing talks, the Mexican trade minister Jaime Serra Puche had his own political imperative in inviting the other delegations to his hometown of Zacatecas for the Mexican-hosted negotiating round. Serra wanted attention to highlight Mexico's role as an emerging player in the international economic policy field and to enhance the ruling party's credentials for Mexico's elections in July 1993. (The Partido Revolucionario Institucional had held a hammerlock on Mexico's politics since the 1910 revolution but maintaining its esteem with up-until-then quiescent voters was still important).

The talks were convened in an elegantly refurbished bullring, the Quinta Real. The hotel had won an award for architectural restoration, and its beautifully appointed rooms were remodelled galleries that used to be part of the "backstage" of the ring itself, which was preserved as a grand plaza. Freed on this occasion from my behind-the-scenes role of tracking negotiations outcomes and translating them into non-specialist language for the eventual communication package, I was tasked to liaise with Canadian media in the absence of Wilson's regular press secretary John Fieldhouse. The assignment could not have been more propitious as it turned out that this round was the one to establish the goals and time-line for the conclusion of the talks.

I participated in a morning session of the three delegations led by Wilson, Serra and Carla Hills, the United States Trade Representative. My pitch to offer up some semblance at least of the positively emerging features of the negotiations was politely declined in favour of simply conveying the three delegations' commitment to achieving a mutually satisfactory agreement. We would at least sincerely express the view that no issues were impeding the countries from reaching a deal. And the outcome at Zacatecas was precisely that: "agreement on a timetable for moving to 'phase two' of the negotiations including preparation of an initial draft text."[5]

It is a decidedly awkward predicament for an ex-journalist charged with the duty of offering less-than-open commentary to former media colleagues about the state of government business, while abiding by officially approved "media lines". A participant in an outreach session I led after the conclusion of NAFTA once suggested that I hadn't been able to decide whether to "run with the fox or hunt with the hounds." At Zacatecas, I seemed to manage this bit of contortionism well, since the headlines following the Zacatecas sessions proclaimed the negotiations as having advanced positively, without criticism of the absence of information about substantial content.

Not revealed in the post-Zacatecas headlines was that the three countries had made key breakthroughs. For all three countries, a vision emerged on how rules-of-origin on autos would work. And each of the countries, offered some flexibility where they had previously taken hard lines: Mexico gave critical ground to opening its energy sector; Canada gave something on opening the garment market while giving the home-grown industry time to adjust; and the US agreed to consider limits on US small-business set-asides and "Buy America" provisions. Most relevant for me was that the three ministers had agreed to conclude negotiations by the summer of 1992. Henceforth our orders were clear. We must assemble the communications package, tracking all key and evolving issues and incorporating them in background material to be ready for press by the summer deadline.

Our work intensified. Beyond describing the agreement provisions in detail, we needed also to explain its effects on all sectors of the economy. For this we would need to rely on Industry Canada, for most sectoral expertise had been shifted from International Trade in recent re-organizations. This was not easy at first. Since the FTA negotiations, the government had been reluctant to make forecasts about what the effects of free trade would be. While offering overall positive assessments of the future, there had been a deep reluctance to make quantifiable estimates. This applied equally to identifying which would be the sectoral impacts of opening the markets.

I had numerous face-to-face meetings with Terry Ford, director of Industry Canada's sectors branch, most of which ended with a quiet resistance to participating in this sector-by-sector analysis. But I persisted, and he eventually yielded to my appeals and agreed to enlist his team in drafting these key documents. Ford's assistance was indispensable, and in the final weeks before the deal, he took time, while staying at his summer cottage, to direct the work of his staff in the CD Howe Building in downtown Ottawa to provide the granular detail the communications package would need.

As importantly, we needed to ensure Minister Wilson's office was happy with the emerging package. What followed was a dogged series of meetings between Daniel, me, Wilson's executive assistant Sheila Riordan and several of the many NAFTA specialist negotiators, to draft layperson's language summaries of virtually every chapter of the agreement. These meetings were nightly at times. Once drafted, each summary would go through numerous "iterations" before arriving at a satisfactory result. This was in the era before e-mail, and it is still vivid in my memory, how I would take the well-worn path, often several times an hour, carrying the latest drafts, from our NAFTA communications offices through the concrete service stairway and the grey-carpeted corridors three floors above to the minister's office atop Tower B. As necessary as this oft-repeated mission was, one could not always be guaranteed a welcome reception. Riordan, who could be friendly, was sometimes stressed by her lynchpin role and could become impatient and abrupt. Still, her blessing was required before our work would eventually be presented to Wilson. From time to time, in our subsequent careers, Sheila and I have run across each other, and our mutual labours over NAFTA in 1992 are among past struggles now fondly remembered. Riordan eventually went on to become the senior political program manager, the diplomatically designated "minister," in Canada's embassy in Washington.

When I did manage to escape headquarters during those interminable months, it was to attend "focus groups" organized by our pollsters. Focus sessions attempt to take the public pulse in a more flexible and nuanced way than strict "question-and-answer" polls. Ten to twelve people, with a variety of demographic backgrounds, are invited to meet in a studio-like setting to discuss around a table the topic that the poll sponsor wants to explore. The polling company provides a facilitator to lead the discussion, and sponsor representatives watch the exchange from behind one-way glass. We asked Angus Reid to conduct several sessions across Canada. I attended several in Ottawa and Winnipeg. These sessions only confirmed me in the determination to produce clear "lay" descriptions of the results of the deal. Economic literacy is not a strong suit for many Canadians. Some focus group participants would become muddled while trying to grapple with the difference between exports and imports. But participants showed a readiness to trust the government if its spokespersons were able to answer their questions in non-specialist language.

The NAFTA talks concluded in a several-week-long negotiating round in Washington DC in July and August, during which time we were on the phone day and night with senior negotiators to track every change – addition or omission – to the evolving agreement. On several occasions we were told to expect the conclusion overnight, but usually that warning would dissolve around 9 or 10 pm. But on Wednesday, August 12, 1992 in the early evening hours, we were advised that indeed the agreement would be completed that night.

I had managed to leave the office early that day and was in a local park working on a community tree-planting project when I received the message. The editors and translators, who had also left for the day, were recalled and what ensued was an all-night marathon involving continuous phone calls with our negotiating team in Washington to get final details, make final edits and translations, format the documents and produce several hundred multi-page packages to be available for the media the following day.

The final product[6] had none of the graphic embellishments or pages of narrative normally associated with government releases on major initiatives. Its format was simple, on plain paper stock and produced by a standard-issue photocopier. But it was fit for purpose – a detailed document to outline the content of the NAFTA, to answer as many questions as we could conceive, and to quell wasteful and erroneous speculation about what Canada's negotiators had agreed to. At 1 pm on Thursday, August 13, the package was presented at a news conference by Minister Wilson in the National Press Gallery theatre.

The following afternoon, several of my colleagues and I were celebrating at a pub in Ottawa's gentrified Glebe district. I distinctly remember hearing on the radio the results of an early poll of reactions to news of the NAFTA deal. Remarkably, 55 per cent of those polled were favourable to the deal. It was the height of summer; the weather in Ottawa was sunny and bright; perhaps Canadians were in a holiday mood. Nonetheless, I felt vindicated for the insistence I had placed from the beginning, informed by my earlier FTA experience, on preparing a full information package for the moment the agreement was reached. And I later noted with satisfaction that from that moment on, in polls on the NAFTA, support rarely dipped below 50 per cent again and would generally trend higher signalling that a significant change had taken place in how Canadians viewed free trade. It took another 18 months for the NAFTA to become law. This included further negotiations on labour and environmental side deals after Bill Clinton was elected US president later that year. And when Jean Chrétien was elected the following year, his incoming Liberal government insisted on some "comfort language" on trade dispute mechanisms, energy and water. Yet the NAFTA that would become the handbook of

North American Trade for the next 25 years was completed in all its core provisions that summer of 1992.

The NAFTA would stand the test of time. Despite the tense negotiations in 2018 with the Trump administration for a revised agreement, most of the essential provisions of the NAFTA were preserved in the newly wrought Canada-Mexico-United States Trade Agreement. Although containing, among other adjustments, more restrictive automotive rules of origin, the agreement still enshrined duty-free trade on the vast majority of the three countries' goods. The all-consuming process to impeach Trump pursued by Congressional Democrats put approval of the revised NAFTA into limbo for months, but it was eventually ratified by Congress and following similar legislative approvals by Canada and Mexico, the new agreement went into force on July 1, 2020.

The original NAFTA epitomized the commitment to free trade and market-oriented solutions to economic management characteristic of the international liberalism of the time. Notwithstanding the fact Canada escaped relatively unscathed, its renegotiation was the consequence of a newly protectionist stance of the United States quite at odds with most previous Republican administrations. But the Trump administration's penchant for waging economic warfare with arbitrary imposition of tariffs exemplified by its trade confrontation with China, portended a new era in world trade built more on raw national interest than multilateralism. It has been accepted as a given for years that for Canada, a modest-sized economy compared to the United States, the European Union and China, multilateralism – and a trading system governed by rules rather than economic power alone – is in the national interest. But some believe that the painstakingly constructed international trading system is in trouble and may not be able to be saved from current trends. I was surprised to encounter one of the Department's retired chief economists at an event in Ottawa in February 2020 proclaiming that the ideal of the multilaterally regulated global market was now old hat. I remembered distinctly that John Curtis had been devoted to the then-orthodoxy of progressively freer trade under agreed trade rules when he oversaw the GATT negotiations that founded the World Trade Organization. In remarks after a speech in Ottawa by Chile's ambassador to Canada, Curtis contended that the old vision was now dead. Ambassador Alejandro Marisio had just concluded a speech vaunting the Canada-Chile free trade agreement and both countries' efforts to continue opening borders in the Pacific Alliance and the Comprehensive and Progressive Agreement for Trans-Pacific Partnership.[7] But Curtis emphasized that teaching his students that bargaining sector-by-sector for national competitive advantage on a largely bilateral basis, rather than for progressive removal of trade barriers multilaterally, will be the name of the game from now on. If Curtis is right, and the old orthodoxy is passé, Canadian tradecraft has a rocky road ahead.

3

Human Security (1994–1999)

It was common in the '90s to refer to the "peace dividend" generated by the end of the Cold War. Resources previously devoted to building nuclear weapons and simultaneously deterring their use, in a balance of terror between the United States and the Soviet Union, could now be deployed to foster peaceful growth. Even the nuclear armaments themselves could be put to use by converting their weapons-grade uranium into fuel for nuclear reactors.

The immediate post-Cold War years were certainly the most optimistic era for international relations in my lifetime. Fears about global warming did not figure in public consciousness as widely as they do today. Islamic fundamentalist terrorism was not the dreaded scourge that would lead to the bolstering of physical security in public places everywhere. China, notwithstanding the political repression, laid bare at Tiananmen in 1989, was charting a course toward economic growth that the rest of the world wanted to participate in. The time had come for Russia and the West to shed their adversarial pasts and become partners. One could envisage Russia becoming a "normal" European country.

The Canadian foreign affairs minister who tried the most to craft a new foreign policy taking advantage of the peace dividend was Lloyd Axworthy. Appointed by Prime Minister Chrétien in 1996, he advocated in his four-year term at the department's helm a new approach to foreign policy which he described as the "human security agenda." It was an inventive way of trying to reconcile "interests" and "values." Diplomatic realists contend that a country's interests form the foundation of its foreign policy. Idealistic pursuit of a policy based on values, such as promoting democracy and human rights, can never prevail over a country's security or commercial needs. Axworthy sought to bridge the gap by arguing that promoting values enhanced the pursuit of our interests.

Axworthy's turn as foreign minister was not the opening act in the Chrétien government's foreign policy performance, however. Chrétien's first minister after 1993 was André Ouellet, the Liberals' Quebec kingpin who had uninterrupted service as an MP since 1967. Ouellet had little experience in, and less affinity for, international relations. His focus seemed to be primarily on how he could use his position to better cement Quebec's attachment to the Liberal party.

Ouellet's ministry proceeded in a desultory manner, with the minister generally following a traditional agenda of bilateral and multilateral engagements without articulating any particular vision. Tellingly, my chief recollection of Ouellet's tenure was an uncomfortable exchange over the appointment of the department's "advertising agent of record." Most departments name an agency that will carry out any necessary advertising to promote its programs and services. The competition had more-than-the usual attractiveness to a would-be contractor since the winner would have access to funds set aside for a so-called, government-wide "jobs and growth agenda." A large portion of this "envelope" would be used to raise the profile of federal services in Quebec. The object: to sway Quebec voters and soften support for sovereignty. Foreign Affairs was implicated in the sense that we were responsible for trade agreements that stimulated trade and boosted the economy, as well as for our Trade Commissioner Service helping firms get access to world markets for goods, services and investment. The "jobs and growth" fund would later come under scrutiny by the federal auditor general and, later, by the Gomery inquiry[1] into the "sponsorship scandal."

Holding a competition for the foreign affairs contract fell under the responsibility of the trade communications division, of which I was acting director at the time. My deputy Paul Fortin managed the competition, which involved three bidders. When Vickers & Benson (in partnership with Quebec firm Groupe Everest) were selected as the winners, I informed minister Ouellet's office of the choice via memo.. Shortly thereafter, I was told that Ouellet was not happy with the choice, would not endorse the recommendation, and would prefer to hold another competition. Fortin, consulting officials at Public Works and Government Services, informed me that, in accordance with government guidelines, the minister did not have the right to second-guess a duly conducted tendering process. It was my job to ensure that Ouellet's office understood, which I did.

My advice was not happily received, and I was asked to reconsider. I said that, following the rules, I could not. I was expecting further pressure but received none. In the following years up until 1999, when the partnership of Groupe Everest and Toronto-based Vickers & Benson was the department's agent of record, the company received contracts for "creative services" amounting to $636,572, and up to $93,000 in commissions for placing advertising, some of it disbursed, under the "jobs and growth agenda."[2] Groupe Everest would be one of five communications agencies named as taking advantage of the funds in the sponsorship program. Gomery saw "no evidence of abusive practices such as billing hours not worked, exaggeration of time charges and over-billing." However, the firm did contribute $194,832 to the Liberal Party of Canada between 1996 and 2003 from revenues at least partly derived from its government contracts. So irrespective of the probity of the tendering procedure that I had to defend, the delivery of Groupe Everest's contract was not without its issues to the degree that Gomery found its management "at best dubious and at worst unethical."[3]

I never learned what would have been Ouellet's preferred advertiser, or even if he had one. It was noted by the Gomery inquiry that Groupe Everest had a particularly close association with Finance Minister Paul Martin who, with little effort to disguise it, was already manoeuvring to unseat Prime Minster Chrétien as Liberal leader. Ouellet, a Chrétien ally, would not have wanted to give material support to a Martin ally. But what I did learn was that a civil servant can draw the line, where warranted, against ministerial wishes. If the result was no gleaming achievement, it was a turf war win under Marquis of Queensbury rules, and the strict procedures that I had followed protected me and my office against any allegations under the sponsorship scandal.

We were soon spared further involvement with Ouellet's curiously domestically focussed foreign policy agenda with the appointment of Lloyd Axworthy to the ministry in January 1996.

Axworthy brought a fresh and innovative approach to the role, predicated on his human security agenda. As a member of the parliamentary press gallery between 1985 and 1990, I had frequently covered Axworthy who, as an MP for Winnipeg, was at the time the lone Liberal voice from western Canada, other than Liberal leader John Turner (Vancouver-Quadra). Axworthy was frequently vilified by his Conservative opponents as having views far to the left of most Canadian voters. But he bristled at this criticism. He maintained his views on foreign policy were founded on the view that individual liberty was paramount, arguing that foreign policy should seek to champion a world order that fostered the safety and prosperity of all citizens. In this he placed himself, he contended, at the heart of classical liberalism which privileged the interests and rights of individuals over the impositions of authoritarian states.

In a speech on human rights and Canadian foreign policy at McGill University in 1997, Axworthy said: "Mature democracies are less likely to go to war with each other, unleash waves of refugees, create environmental catastrophes, or engage in terrorism. Jobs and growth at home are increasingly dependent on trade and investment abroad. States that protect human rights and the rule of law are more likely to honour their commercial commitments. The health of the international economy is linked to issues of stability and security. All of this means that respect for human rights is an imperative of living in a global society."[4]

In the numerous news releases and backgrounders that the communications section churned out for Axworthy, the link to the human security agenda was a unifying theme. Taken to its limit, this agenda incorporated the "responsibility to protect" which postulated, in a major theoretical innovation in foreign policy, that the international community could be permitted to interfere in a country's domestic affairs if its government was trampling on its own citizens' human rights. This new doctrine did not arise just from philosophical musing. The world had witnessed two horrifying genocides that were grotesque affronts to the peaceful hopes of the post-Cold War era. Neither in Rwanda nor in Bosnia did international institutions or other individual states do much of concrete value to save those two countries' citizens from mass murder. The climate was such that another crisis in the Balkans persuaded concerned countries to put the "responsibility to protect" doctrine to the test.

In Kosovo, a province of Serbia, armed forces attempting to suppress the separatist movement of the Albanian-speaking majority, had widened their efforts to round up and kill civilians. The same techniques that the Serbians had deployed against Bosnia were now being used against the Kosovar population. The massacres of Sarajevo were too fresh in people's minds for a reprise of these events in Kosovo to be ignored. In October 1998, the United Nations Security Council approved resolution 1203 (with abstentions from Russia and China) that called on the Serbian government to reach a peaceful agreement with Kosovar authorities to provide the province with greater autonomy and accept a NATO and Organization of Security and Cooperation in Europe (OSCE) monitoring mission.

NATO's action began on March 23, 1999. I was summoned to represent the communications bureau at the daily Kosovo interdepartmental task force meetings that would be held daily during the war (I had recently been re-assigned from trade to foreign policy communications). The task force was headed by Paul Heinbecker, assistant deputy minister responsible for international security. Tall, calm and serious, with occasional glimpses of wry wit, Heinbecker oversaw the daily proceedings, conducting a *tour d'horizon* with officials from all departments present, in particular defence and the solicitor general's department (before the post-9/11 creation of the more powerful public safety ministry). Also included was the Canadian International Development Agency (CIDA) whose resources could be called upon to offer humanitarian relief. (Heinbecker would later be appointed Canada's ambassador to the UN, where he would have to handle Canada's stance in opposition to the US-instigated war in Iraq in 2003). His right hand was Jim Wright, director-general in the security branch. Wright possessed a kind of youthful sincerity, and was always articulate and measured in speech, which made him the perfect candidate to give the daily press briefings he had been tasked to deliver, alongside spokespeople of the armed forces, at department of national defence headquarters. He and Heinbecker elicited from task force members the latest situation reports and then summarized the state of play. It was then my role to work with my communications officers and department policy experts to develop the day's key messages for delivery at Wright's briefing. Stewart Wheeler, who would much later become the department's chief of protocol, worked in the media office at the time and was the liaison between Wright and the communications team.

NATO troops launched a bombing campaign based on a UN resolution despite Chinese and Russian abstentions. This represented a communications challenge throughout the conflict. Resolution 1203 demanded that the Federal Republic of Yugoslavia (at that time essentially the government of Serbia) comply with previous resolutions giving autonomy to the people of Kosovo and refrain from violence in suppressing them. Unlike the UN resolution that gave authorization in 1989 to intervention in Iraq, the Kosovo resolution contained no reference to the use of "all necessary means" – the code for taking military action. Nonetheless, Canada took the view that NATO's action took political, if not technically explicit, legitimacy from UN authority. This position was principally inspired by the desire – and in fact, the humanitarian necessity – to protect the Kosovar population from forced exile and murder by Serbian forces. Recent history was on NATO's side. NATO bombings of Serb forces surrounding Sarajevo in 1995, after years of hand-wringing about what to do to protect Bosnians from clearly genocidal attacks, pushed back the Serbian force and led at last to a peace deal in the Dayton Accord. If the slaughter was stopped in Bosnia then it could also be stopped in Kosovo.

My recollection of those days evokes a dissonance between the atmosphere in Ottawa and the reality of what was happening in the theatre of war. The task force would gather daily in the 8th-floor conference room of the Pearson A tower. The room has a panoramic view of the Rideau River, surrounding green space and the church towers overlooking the historic Bytown market. Spring was early that year and the morning sun flooded the east-facing conference room uplifting spirits after what had been a typically grey Ottawa winter. Normally there would be a sense of renewal and optimism. Yet we were dealing with a situation where lives were in the balance, not only the Kosovars' but also those of their Serbian foes and the NATO and allied forces deployed to the region.

As in the case of the Persian Gulf War, the main Canadian contribution to the Kosovo campaign was from the air force, which had deployed 18 CF-18s to the theatre. Their role, in this case, was purposefully aggressive, unlike the support role to which they were consigned in the Gulf. The aircraft would be directly involved in attacks on the Serbian forces. In a two-and-a-half-month campaign, the Canadian fighter-bombers made 678 sorties into Kosovar and Serbian airspace. Using precision-guided bombs of either 500- or 2000-pounds, the aircraft attacked Serbian ground artillery and critical Serbian-controlled infrastructure. In keeping with a NATO agreement, the nationality of the NATO aircraft in each identified sortie was kept secret with the purpose that in theory at least all participating countries would share collective responsibility. The campaign ended on June 10 with Slobodan Milosevic's Serbian government agreeing to withdraw its troops from Kosovo and accept the establishment of a UN-backed OSCE mission to assume administrative powers over Kosovo and organize a civilian government.

From a communications perspective, our readiness to respond to negative public reactions to the war served us well. Wright's daily briefings were forthcoming and informative. He was always well versed in the events of the day and tied them always to Canada's "human security" perspective. Ultimately, we were to encounter little public pushback during the 58-day campaign. Few celebrated the pictures of the precision-guided bombing that destroyed bridges, roads and military ground squadrons. They were a sobering reality of the war. The most controversial event was the misdirected bombing of the building housing the Chinese embassy in Belgrade by US aircraft, killing three Chinese journalists and injuring 20 others.

Still, the war stirred little resistance among the majority of the Canadian public. The policy of not naming the pilots who carried out the daily sorties into Kosovo and Bosnian airspace made it difficult for the military spokespeople to underline the contributions Canada made to the campaign.[5] Still, opinion polls conducted by Compass, Angus Reid and Environics at different stages of the war showed that 60 per cent of those polled backed the government's position and its actions.[6] The demonstrated impotence of the international community in the face of the Rwanda and Bosnian genocides had prepared the way for the public's endorsement of definitive action in the face of a clear humanitarian threat to a civilian population. In addition, the past success of the 1990 Persian Gulf War had shown that military actions could achieve clearly defined results.

This would be perhaps the high tide of support for the "responsibility to protect" doctrine. A subsequent bombing campaign over Libya during the so-called Arab Spring in 2011, invoked the R2P doctrine, but its results were a years-long civil war resulting in widespread bloodshed and a refugee crisis that had stretched Europe's ability to cope with a wave of uncontrolled immigration. Although not waged under R2P, the quagmire of the war in Iraq (in which Canada famously did not participate), the unending conflict in Afghanistan and the horrors of the civil war in Syria, made the public leery of armed interventions, whether or not "responsibility to protect" could be justifiably invoked. This innovative doctrine has become a suspect instrument. As urgent as is the need to protect civilians, the means of doing so is vexed by political and military realities, including the relative strengths of states and their militaries, and social and geographical conditions. Responsibility to protect is a doctrine that must find its way through the *realpolitik* of the day.

If R2P failed to duplicate anywhere its qualified success in Kosovo, there were other initiatives that Canada undertook to enhance human security in the post-Cold War world. Perhaps the most significant of the accomplishments of Axworthy's ministry was the successful negotiation of the Convention on the Prohibition on the Use, Stockpiling, Production and Transfer of Anti-Personnel Mines and on Their Destruction, otherwise known as the Ottawa Convention. Not all initiatives share such success, while others well-intended do not achieve their initial promise.

Today, it seems almost bitterly nostalgic to invoke it, but the emergence of the G8, adding Russia to the existing G7 comprising the United States, Germany, Japan, France, the UK, Italy and Canada, provided the forum for previously unheard-of cooperation. For example, the United States and Russia agreed to reduce their nuclear arsenals and destroy unwanted warheads.

Canada was able to play a part. During the Moscow Summit on Nuclear Safety and Security in April 1996, Prime Minister Chrétien announced that Canada had agreed in principle that plutonium from dismantled US and Russian nuclear weapons could be tested for use as fuel in Canadian reactors.

The practical application of this agreement would take time. But in due course, Natural Resources Canada (NRCan) and Atomic Energy Canada Ltd. (AECL) would propose to take small quantities of Russian and US enriched uranium for tests in the CANDU nuclear reactor in

Chalk River, Ontario. The tests would be the precursor to larger imports of plutonium, in a mixed oxide form known as MOX, to be used to power Ontario Hydro's Bruce Nuclear Reactor.

I was drawn into the communications planning for the experimental MOX test. Our role was to ensure that the foreign policy aspects of this undertaking would be clearly understood by the public. The project must be seen not as a purely commercial transaction but as having a higher purpose in aiding nuclear disarmament. We were to emphasize that the fuel was coming from nuclear missiles or bombs which were being dismantled to reduce their numbers in both US and Soviet arsenals, to further the long-term goals of arms control.

Worthy goals notwithstanding, controversy always stalks anything to do with nuclear material and the real dangers associated with radioactivity. AECL and NRCan had identified the routes along which the MOX fuel would be carried to Chalk River. The US material was to cross the Canadian border at Sault Ste-Marie, Ontario, and the Russian material, shipped by sea, would enter Canada at Cornwall, Ontario. From those two ports of entry, the MOX would be carried along a variety of Ontario highways to reach Chalk River.

The two agencies launched a detailed process to consult all the communities along the route to assure them that the shipments would be safe. Those assurances rested largely on how the material would be physically sealed. Larry Shewchuk, the spokesperson for AECL said: "The shipment will contain 528 grams of weapons-derived plutonium contained in 14.5 kilograms of ceramic MOX fuel pellets housed inside 28 Zircaloy (zirconium alloy) seal-welded metal tubes." The message was that the fuel was fully sealed in impenetrable containers that would not break apart even in the most violent highway accident. During the summer of 1999, we awaited word of the arrival of the material and the imminent transport by road across Ontario.

Many dedicated federal employees have devoted their careers to public affairs, and to its subset of strategic communications. The best exhibit a *sang-froid* that helps them respond coolly to the eruption of unexpected controversy. They show flexibility before sudden policy shifts, especially with changes of the political party in power.

From the time I entered the government, I knew that public policy itself – as distinct from the explanation or the promotion of it – offered different challenges. Communications staff need to find the best ways to articulate what the government is doing, but do not have the opportunity to shape it. And at times, there can be the sense that communications are not clearly explaining government policies and actions as much as they are offering an often-insincere gloss to them.

In late 1999, we were still waiting for instructions to initiate communications for the transport of the MOX fuel to Chalk River. NRCan and AECL had advised that the shipment might not take place that year, due to the early winter closure of the St. Lawrence Seaway. We were preparing to put the information campaign on hold. Then with no notice, all team members were informed that AECL had received approval for the shipment to be *flown* by helicopter to Chalk River, an action for which there had been no prior consultation.

I have never been able to determine whether the air transport option had been under consideration all along. But I had the sense that the elaborate plans for road shipment and the extensive public consultation with the various communities affected were a ruse to divert attention from the actual plan. I have subsequently confirmed that false leads and decoys are commonly used in plans to transport hazardous materials. In any event, I had participated in a process that – for good or ill – had misled many of my federal colleagues, activist organizations, and the public at large. And in the end, after some initial experiments, the MOX initiative was suspended. There were considerable technical challenges to adapting it to use in Canadian reactors. Scaling up the process to produce viable quantities of MOX fuel would require major capital investments at Chalk River that would prove to be economically prohibitive. That, along with the mostly public affairs vulnerabilities associated with transport into and out of Chalk River, led eventually to the quiet shelving of the project. Despite this anticlimactical ending, however, the plan to convert weapons uranium to reactor fuel has not been entirely abandoned. Despite the now-fractious relationship between Russia and the United States, some American reactors are consuming some de-commissioned Russian material. And

Canada's SNC Lavalin, which took over AECL, has proposed building CANDU reactors in the UK to help rid Britain of 140 million tonnes of weapons-grade plutonium that was produced in surplus to the small nuclear arsenal that that country still possesses.[7]

When the MOX flight took place, I had already negotiated my next career move to the department's trade policy branch. I was moving from communications to what is sometimes referred to as "policy operations," and was looking forward to the new role. The sudden change of plans for the MOX flight to Chalk River helped me not to regret the change. In the years to come, I would be dealing not with geopolitical outcomes of the post-Cold War, but with the evolving role of trade policy under the prevailing free-market order governed by internationally negotiated rules.

4

Freedoms of the Skies (2000–2006)

The man's voice on the long-distance line was anxious, incredulous. "Is it true that we cannot fly tonight? Our flights are banned from Canadian airspace?" He was a representative of a Russian air freight service that had carved itself a niche offering commercial flights of the world's largest cargo planes, Russian-designed and-built Antonovs. It was a Friday night in late-October 2002. Indeed, the Russian government *had* been advised, by official diplomatic note, that all Russian commercial services were banned from Canadian airspace. The airline representative was concerned about a cargo flight scheduled that evening between a Russian city and Chicago.

My duty: to communicate without qualification that all Russian flights over Canada must stop, regardless of the millions of dollars of business at risk and regardless of the number of passengers who would be inconvenienced. I was frightened of what could happen if the Russian didn't take me seriously. My only instrument was a flimsy piece of paper, a diplomatic note. A copy was in the hands of the Russian government, and another was in the hands of Canada's air traffic controllers responsible for monitoring traffic through Canadian airspace. The Russian and I didn't talk of what would happen if the commercial flight went ahead. But the prospect of a couple of Canadian CF-18 fighter-bombers sent aloft to intercept the plane filled me with dread. My Russian interlocutor should feel the same. I hoped so, but I didn't know for sure.

I joined the department's trade policy services bureau in late 1999 after nearly a decade in strategic communications. Through my work on NAFTA and other trade files, I had developed a strong rapport with managers in the trade policy bureau, and they asked if I might want to switch to a "policy operations" role. After years of polishing communications lines and offering advice to ministers' offices that was embraced at times but frequently ignored, I was up for a new challenge. What was available was a position in air transport policy that involved negotiations at the World Trade Organization and the Montreal-based International Civil Aviation Organization (ICAO), but more tangibly, negotiations to secure air traffic rights between Canada and other countries. Opening to me was a whole new world of agreements, disputes, conventions and rules governing the operations of the world's international aviation services.

It is indeed a specialized world, which falls outside the mainstream of trade negotiations at both the multilateral (WTO) and bilateral (country-to-country) levels. Separate treatment of air services dates to the end of the Second World War, when the allies who were designing the new international institutional architecture, agreed that air transport services had a special place that derived from sovereignty over a country's own airspace. Occupying an enormous territory that carriers need access to for efficient polar routes between the United States, Europe and Asia, Canada enjoys out-size leverage in this realm. Under bilateral agreements for commercial flights, countries agree to let flights go *to, from, through* and *beyond* their skies, but Canada never agreed, as most other countries have – to cede the right to *transit*, or fly over, national territory without stopping. We reserved this geographic advantage, and in the case of the Russian flights, we had decided to put that advantage to use.

We'd been brought to this juncture by Russia's decision to deny Air Canada rights Canadian officials believed it had. Moscow would not let the airline offer direct passenger flights through Russian airspace from Toronto to Delhi, India. Of course, Russia's skies are even more extensive than Canada's. But the bilateral air transport agreement that Canada had signed years ago with Russia, did, in Canada's view, provide specific over-flight rights. Russia was contravening the agreement by denying them. The motive was obvious to all. The Russian airline Aeroflot was doing a brisk business flying passengers from Toronto to Delhi via a stop in Moscow. Russia did not want this lucrative business undermined by Air Canada offering non-stop flights directly between Toronto and the Indian capital. To be economical, these flights would have to go through Russian polar airspace

I was surprised at how aggressive Foreign Affairs' senior management was prepared to be in recommending a response to the Russian position.

My initial consultation with John Gero, assistant deputy minister of trade policy, took place in passing in the hallway. He said with no hesitation we should be prepared to block all Russian overflights. Gero, always plainspoken, said "shut 'em down," or words to that effect. I advised my colleagues at Transport Canada how far Foreign Affairs officials were prepared to go, and we duly drafted a recommendation to then-Foreign Affairs Minister Bill Graham to threaten the closure of Canadian airspace to Russian commercial services. When he saw the memo, Graham immediately grasped that closure would be an extraordinary measure sure to offend the Russians with whom in those days we had relatively good relations. Although Vladimir Putin had recently become the Russian president, there was still hope at the time of Russia becoming more integrated into the western economic and political system. Canadian perception of Putin's government was not that of the reactionary and authoritarian power that would later provoke civil war in eastern Ukraine, invade Crimea, kill opposition leaders, ex-spies and journalists at home and abroad and eventually launch a war of unimaginable brutality against Ukraine as a whole. At the end of a meeting with Foreign Affairs' chief air negotiator John McNab, Graham expressed trepidation about what we were about to do, but he took the leap. Russia would be told that Canadian airspace was closed to its commercial aviation as of midnight Universal Time on Friday, October 21, 2003.

That evening I was with McNab in our tower C, sixth-floor offices. I advised him of my call with the Russian airline rep, and we went online to a flight-tracking application to monitor the cargo flight, as well as a scheduled Moscow-Toronto Aeroflot passenger flight. The cargo flight did not appear on the screen, but the Aeroflot flight did. About mid-way across the Atlantic approaching Canadian airspace, the flight detoured to the south, then made an unusual right-angle turn parallel with New York City. Aeroflot had apparently decided to land in New York, then put Canadian-destined passengers on other airlines' flights into Toronto. We breathed a sigh of relief. The Russians had complied with the ban.

We had given the Russian authorities fair warning. They were notified weeks in advance of our plan to suspend their services. Our embassy in Moscow had been in contact with the Russian foreign ministry to advise them. A stern protest came from Sergei Kislyak, deputy minister of foreign affairs (who would much later become notorious as the Russian ambassador to Washington, with whom Jared Kushner sought the contentious back channel to Vladimir Putin for his father-in-law, Donald Trump, in the lead-up to Trump's inauguration as president). Thus, our initial advisories led to the convening of a negotiating session in Montreal to try to resolve the matter. We found ourselves across the table from Alexander Neradko, Russia's first deputy minister of transport, who had an uncanny resemblance to Omar Sharif in the 1967 film *Doctor Zhivago*. Neradko inveighed against "the surprising, strange and unCanadian approach of deadlines and ultimatums." But he offered no concrete suggestions to resolve the issue. Perhaps he thought that we would be shamed into changing our minds by his assessment of our "harsh measures." What he did point out was that Canada was routinely using 63 weekly commercial overflights of Russia, while Russia used only 18 over Canada, in addition to its four weekly passenger flights between Moscow and Toronto. The clear implication was that Russia was prepared to retaliate.

The Montreal talks went nowhere, and we implemented the ban. Startled by our determination, the Russians asked us to meet them on "neutral ground" in Paris where we faced off against the particularly intractable Sergei Vasiliev, the deputy director of international affairs of the Russian state civil aviation authority. We advised that the proscription of overflights would remain in place until Air Canada was granted the rights that we believed the existing bilateral treaty gave them. Aeroflot's loss of the Toronto-Moscow-Delhi service was starting to take its toll, and in exchange for an agreement to resume negotiations in Moscow, the Russians agreed temporarily to grant (in our view, restore) overflight rights to Air Canada until February 29, 2004. In turn we would lift the overflights ban.

I was frankly looking forward to visiting Moscow for the talks scheduled for December 9 to 11, 2003. Russia occupied a large space in my imagination. Not unusual or surprising for so many of us who grew up in the Cold War in the shadow of "mutually assured destruction," the always imminent horror that was supposed to deter the West and the Soviet Union from launching a nuclear war against each other. As part of civil defence, air raid sirens were erected throughout the city of Calgary where I grew up. I would gasp at the alarms of ambulances and fire trucks thinking that missiles were in mid-flight. So naturally one wanted to know "the enemy:" the history of the October 1917 revolution; the inevitable descent into authoritarianism of the Leninist project; Stalin's years of terror; the Soviet Union's indomitable stance against the Nazi invaders; the lowering of the Iron Curtain and the origins of the east-west nuclear standoff. As I pursued my research, I was introduced to the great literary works of Dostoevsky, Pasternak and Solzhenitsyn. I loved the musical works of Tchaikovsky, Prokofiev, and Shostakovich. I had even studied Russian for a couple of years in high school. Ultimately, the emergence of Mikhail Gorbachev and his policies of *glasnost* (openness) and *perestroika* (perestroika) that led to the end of the Cold War seemed an historic miracle. And as a journalist in the late '80s, I was introduced during a reception in Ottawa to Gorbachev's remarkable foreign minister, Eduard Shevardnadze, who forsook the ideological bounds of Cold War diplomacy to seek a new framework based on the "principles of good, justice, humanism, and spirituality."[1] The promise of Gorbachev's policies faded quickly in the wake of the hardships wrought by the collapse of central planning and its replacement by the buccaneer capitalism of the oligarchs. Yet in visiting Moscow, I would be going to a place that filled a large part of my imagination. Partly because of this, I wanted my soon-to-be fiancée to join me on this journey.

It is not common for officials to take their companions with them during negotiations, but it was acceptable from time to time provided one paid personally for their travel. I asked Suzanne, who I had been seeing for more than a year, to accompany me and she agreed. While I was attending negotiation sessions, she would have the opportunity to see some of Moscow's sights. I had also arranged a day of leave at either end of the talks so that we could tour some of the city together. Since she would be traveling with the Canadian delegation, she was listed on the diplomatic note to the Russian embassy seeking the necessary visas. Soon, we became aware that Putin's Russia had not abandoned some of the Soviet Union's Cold War behaviours.

At a downtown currency exchange to swap dollars for rubles, a gentleman stepped into line behind Suzanne and started quizzing her about her travel plans. Outgoing and sociable by nature, Suzanne engaged in a conversation and spoke plainly of her planned visit to Moscow. After she obtained her rubles from the cashier, her acquaintance disappeared. When she told me about the encounter, I suspected that the man in line was an officer of the Russian embassy gathering intelligence, seeking to find out what covert role Suzanne might be playing on the delegation. To have known when she was to visit the foreign exchange office, the officer would have had to have access to our phone and email correspondence, or have physically spied on her movements around Ottawa, or both. I assumed from then on that after we arrived in Moscow, it would be very likely that we would be watched, and our accommodation bugged.

We landed in Moscow in winter weather very similar to what we had left behind in Ottawa: -15 degrees and light snow. After enduring a long line at customs and immigration, presided over by a grim and uncommunicative border agent, we took a cab to the Aerostar Hotel in a northern suburb of Moscow, adjacent to the offices of the Russian civil aviation authority and one of Moscow's metro lines. The Aerostar had once been owned by the Canadian IMP group in a partnership with Aeroflot that had not run smoothly. At one point, IMP had seized, by Canadian court order, an Aeroflot aircraft's fuel at a Canadian airport to press its partner to pay the money it owed. Later (but after our stay in Moscow), the hotel was physically commandeered by an armed "business organization" and forcibly put under new ownership.

There was nothing physically exceptional about the Aerostar. It could have taken the place of a Holiday Inn near any North American airport. However, we discovered it had an exceptional restaurant with one of the most elaborate buffets, including ample fresh seafood and caviar, that I had ever seen. Guests on the day of our arrival were serenaded by a live musical ensemble offering traditional balalaika music. Tackling Moscow's exceptional metro system, relying on my dim memory of the Cyrillic alphabet, Suzanne and I made our way to Red Square where we were kept away from Lenin's tomb by armed guards. The embalmed body of the Soviet Union's founder was under repair - again. But we spent part of the afternoon in the GUM, the legendary shopping centre across from the Kremlin, and later walked by St Basil's across the Moscow River and found the marvellous Tretyakov Museum of Russian art.

The negotiations began the following day and our delegation, including representatives of Transport Canada, the Canadian Transportation Agency and observers from Air Canada, trudged across the snowy parking lot of the civil aviation authority. There was an immediate change in the tenor of the talks compared to earlier rounds. Neradko was nowhere to be seen, and although the "nyet"-wielding Vasiliev was present, the Russian delegation was led by Vitaly Pavliuk, the head of the civil aviation authority, who was from the outset civil and gentlemanly. Pavliuk had risen to his position not through the old Soviet bureaucracy but through his lifelong profession as an aircraft pilot who'd acquired hours of flying time in the Russian far north. At least the atmospherics would be more pleasant as our negotiator, McNab, always distinguished by his impeccable manners, seemed to hit it off with Pavliuk.

Still, the stuff of talks continued to be difficult. What had only been mentioned peripherally in earlier encounters – the technical capacity of Russia to monitor and direct high-altitude traffic through its airspace – became suddenly a high priority issue. We were dubious about Russians' claims that their navigation systems could be overwhelmed by the too frequent passage of aircraft on high Arctic routes. Air Canada was accompanied by an expert in technical navigation issues, but he wasn't able to verify, or refute, the Russian claims on the spot.

At the same time, it became increasingly apparent that Pavliuk had a mandate to offer a partial deal that would provisionally authorize Air Canada to fly its Toronto-Delhi route without conceding that the airline already had this right within the Canada-Russia agreement. As much as the offer might settle the immediate issue at hand, it would not allow other Canada-Russia flights by Air Canada and other airlines, which would be of value in the future.

In every instance in which a Canadian delegation negotiates air traffic rights, it does so in accordance with a cabinet-approved mandate. No deal can be reached without its falling into the parameters set out. While our mandate would not permit us to accept the Russians' offer to authorize the single Air Canada route, it was a significant enough development that we needed to bring it to our masters in Ottawa. Under the direction of the foreign affairs and transport ministers, the mandate could be modified in consultation with other members of cabinet. Wary that our communications on open lines would be monitored, we asked our embassy for access to its secure room to make the call.

Canada's embassy in Moscow is in an early 19th-century *art nouveau* building on Starkonynushenny Lane in one of the city's central, historical districts. In 2003, the embassy maintained a certain outward dignity, but behind the outer walls, it consisted of an improvised rabbit warren of offices supplemented by a modular building in an old courtyard. The site was too small to accommodate all the embassy staff comfortably, yet after years of negotiations, a series of Canadian ambassadors had been unable to win from the Russians a new site on which to build a more modern chancery. What the embassy did have was a deep basement which I recall being at least two storeys underground where there was a secure conference room through which secret communications could be conducted with Ottawa. Physically sealed with an airlock entrance, the tiny room was remarkably stuffy, but we were able to make phone contact with secure phones in the ministers' offices in Ottawa. Adding to the oppressive atmosphere that day was news earlier in the day of a terrorist incident near Red Square where a suicide bomber had blown herself up "killing at least five others and seriously wounding 13"[2] outside the National Hotel. Suzanne was supposed to have met a guide arranged for her by the Aerostar Hotel to visit public spaces in the Kremlin. Mercifully, the incident occurred before her scheduled rendezvous, but the planned tour was called off for the day.

Our interlocutors on the other end of the line included a senior staffer from Minister Graham's office and Transport Canada's director-general of international air relations, and they were supportive of McNab's assessment that the Russian partial offer was not enough. Rather than obtain only the immediate objective of approval of Air Canada's India flight, we wanted to ensure existing rights in the agreement would be honoured in other instances, and we wanted to permanently expand Canadian access to other countries through Russian air space. We needed to consult our airline stakeholders as well. Air Canada's observer on the delegation was Yves Dufresne, the airline's head of international agreements. Although the Russian offer would have met the airline's short-term objective, he agreed with the delegation's determination to obtain a comprehensive solution. The decision was to adhere to the existing mandate, and we returned to the table to tell Pavliuk that his offer was far from enough.

I don't believe Pavliuk was surprised by our rejection of the temporary fix. Both sides had agreed to settle the dispute before or by February 29, and at this stage, 2½ months remained. We left Moscow empty-handed but were confident in the Russians' willingness to convene other rounds. We met the Russians again in early January in Ottawa for what seemed to be an effort by them to apply further pressure to settle for a temporary deal. The Russian delegation remained intransigent, not willing to give any ground toward recognition of a Canadian right to over-fly Russian airspace.

When we met in Moscow again toward the end of February, both sides remained fixed on their positions until the end of the second day of the scheduled three-day round. Before we were to wrap up for the evening, Pavliuk invited McNab to a tête-à-tête in which, after some social back and forth, the Russian negotiator conceded Russia's willingness to craft a comprehensive deal.

I do not know definitively to this day what brought about the Russians' change of heart. Certainly, McNab had evinced the Canadian determination to obtain a comprehensive solution and had done so throughout with has characteristic courtesy, not once resorting to the expressions of frustration and anger that some negotiators think – usually incorrectly – will knock their adversaries off their game. The fact that remained lurking in the background was that the dispute had begun with Canada blocking lucrative Russian commercial operations to Canada and through our airspace. The Russians were appalled that we had done this in the first place. There was the fear that we would do so again. It would have been the logical outcome of failed negotiations.

But there was also negotiations fatigue. A revised agreement always has the advantage that no one will be compelled to return to the negotiating table in short order; there are always other bilateral agreements waiting in the wings that need attention. In any event, Canada's ambassador Chris Westdal, who had several years of experience trying to win Moscow's approval for a new Canadian embassy site as well as Russian obduracy on other issues, was impressed. When we arrived in his office the following day to provide a full briefing on the successful talks, Westdal greeted McNab with jocular extravagance: "See, the conquering hero comes!" Air Canada was grateful for the agreement achieved. I was happy that we wouldn't have to return to banning Russian overflights, armed only with the wording of a one-page diplomatic note.

Every bilateral air negotiation has a limited menu. Which airlines will be designated to use the routes? Which cities will be served? How many flights will be authorized? What size aircraft, carrying how many passengers, will be approved? Will there be any limits on the fares to be charged? And what "freedoms" will be permitted from the official "freedoms" roster. The first freedom is to fly over; the second is to stop for technical reasons; the third is to fly to, and the fourth is to fly back. The fifth freedom allows an airline to pick up another country's passengers en route to somewhere else. And the sixth freedom allows an airline to bring passengers to its own country and then carry them on to another.

Many trade theorists find bilateral agreements archaic. In keeping with the then prevailing wisdom that world markets should allow free and open competition, theorists would advocate an international convention to permit any airline to serve any route at any time, subject to the rules and regulations for safe air travel devised by the International Civil Aviation Organization (ICAO). Such an approach has met strong resistance from most countries jealous of their ability to direct traffic through their sovereign air spaces. A handful of countries, subscribing to a principled free-market approach are prepared unilaterally to open their skies, although in practice such access is often withheld pending offsetting concessions. Canada under the Harper Conservatives flirted with such an approach. But its "blue sky" policy declared, as had other countries who had theoretically declared open skies, that this was conditional on satisfactory reciprocal concessions. The limits of the Conservatives' aspirational policy were made obvious when the government refused Persian Gulf carriers from the United Arab Emirates and Qatar unrestricted flights into Toronto, which would have flooded the Canadian market with Asian-origin traffic. It is difficult to compete with airlines that have access to an unlimited source of interest-free petrodollars, even if the airlines insist that they are not subsidized by their home governments.

Notwithstanding the general tendency to open markets up, the mercantilist bilateral approach promoting the interests of national carriers still prevails in many markets. In a sense, the interest of the carriers embodies the national interest. Having greater access to and from all destinations at economical prices, and in so doing strengthening the economy is a high priority. But preserving a strong, domestically based airline industry is for most countries a caveat attached to that aspiration. Negotiations are usually set according to commercial priorities, meaning that large markets which offered the most potential to Canadian airlines would receive the most attention. But there are exceptions.

In the fall of 2000, we received an offer from the Caribbean island of Aruba to negotiate an agreement. Aruba is part of the Kingdom of the Netherlands but granted *status aparte*, making it "a country of its own,"[3] within the kingdom. This means that Aruba is sovereign in all things except foreign affairs and defence. Serge April, who was the chief negotiator at the time, wasted little time in declining this invitation. We simply had other priorities. Yet within days of his reply, the Arubans came back saying that, without an agreement, they would have no choice but to cancel the only passenger service currently flying between Aruba and Canada – Air Transat's thrice weekly seasonal charter between Toronto and Reina Beatrix Airport in Oranjestad, the Aruban capital. The revenue generated by three weekly flights of Boeing 737s carrying roughly 150 passengers each, operating from October to May was significant. This was business Air Transat was loath to lose. Therefore, the company urged us to accept the Aruban invitation. But given that the island's foreign relations were reserved for the Netherlands, could we legally accept the offer? Copious messages were exchanged with our embassies in Venezuela, officially accredited[4] to Aruba, and in the Netherlands. Although there was some ambiguity, our colleagues determined that Aruba had the right to negotiate treaties in the commercial realm, although they ultimately must be formally approved by the Dutch foreign ministry.

After these dilatory discussions over jurisdiction, the Arubans were starting to lose patience. They threatened again to cancel Air Transat's rights. We swiftly saw the light of reason. A week spent in Aruba at the beginning of February, with Ottawa almost certainly in a deep freeze, was enticing. The island is tucked into the far southwestern corner of the Caribbean, a few degrees north of the equator. With average temperatures in the high 20s, little rainfall and the constant moderating effects of the warm trade winds, it is a tourist mecca. It's a prosperous and safe island, with a population of slightly more than 100,00 people and a GDP per capita of more than $25,000 annually, placing it in the upper tier of world economies. The people constitute a blend of Indigenous Caribbean, Portuguese, Spanish, English, and Dutch who have developed their distinct language, Papiamento. There were no hindrances to flying there for a week of talks.

After taking Air Transat's regular flight to Aruba, we found the negotiations were amicable and easy. By late in the week, we had drafted a text that contained a remarkably open set of traffic rights. Frequently, agreements will be wholly symmetrical with the rights of one party being equal to those of the other. In this case, all the airlines of each country could access all destinations in the other. But since Aruba had no airlines and only one destination, this meant that Canadian airlines were able to offer as many flights as they wished from any Canadian city, without competition. Of course, this all made sense because Aruba's interest, in addition to the theoretical one of exercising its sovereign authority, was to encourage as much tourism as possible to their island "paradise." The results of this agreement are plain today. A quick survey of the web shows that airlines offer two flights daily from Toronto and one each from Montreal, Vancouver, Calgary, and Ottawa. Such outcomes underline that although air transport agreements are rooted in archaic mercantilism, they can certainly be spurs to market-driven tourism, investment and trade.

The terrorist attack on New York's World Trade Centre on September 11, 2001 bore heavily on our work. I was reviewing overnight email correspondence in my office when I heard the director of the trade services policy division shout as he ran through the halls that an aircraft had struck one of the towers. A little mystified at first, thinking of a small aircraft in an unfortunate aviation accident, I was soon disabused of that notion as I watched news come in on the TV in the chief negotiator's office. Our office's role was but an afterthought that day as the locus of the federal government's attention was concentrated in the air traffic control system managed by Transport Canada and NavCanada, whose air traffic controllers were shutting the country's airspace down. It was many weeks before we resumed negotiations of bilateral air agreements after a lengthy hiatus in which even the future of a robust international aviation industry was being questioned. The extraordinary security measures implemented following the attacks still cast a shadow.

Most prominently for us in those days were considerations related to the agreement to operate flights between Canada and Lebanon. Air Canada had long wanted to take advantage of the pent-up demand for flights between the two countries, especially among Canada's large Lebanese population, centred in Montreal and Ottawa. The standing agreement predicated the opening of flights on a review of security issues which, for the most part, involved providing assurances that flights into and out of Beirut's international airport were not vulnerable to hijackings, hostage-takings or terrorist attacks. Air Canada pointed out repeatedly that European carriers were operating regularly in and out of Beirut. In fact, Canadian Lebanese-bound passengers were being carried to European airline hubs to be transferred to European airlines flying from Frankfurt, Amsterdam, or Paris. Air Canada considered this situation a significant lost opportunity. Sympathetic to the airline's position, we, trade negotiators at Foreign Affairs and the international relations group at Transport Canada, pushed for a security audit of Beirut airport which Transport Canada in collaboration with the Canada Border Services Agency agreed to do. Twice, Canadian teams visited the airport to conduct their reviews and twice concluded that the airport's security measures met the highest international standards. They offered no objection to the implementation of regular passenger service between Montreal and Beirut.

Plans were well underway for the service to begin in June 2003 when I received a phone call from the director of the department's international security division, Ruth Archibald (soon to become high commissioner to South Africa). She advised me that she had received a message from US officials in Washington expressing grave concerns over the pending Canada-Lebanon flights. Among their worries was that the Beirut airport was located in the Hezbollah-controlled section of the Lebanese capital and, irrespective of tight security procedures, the airport was vulnerable to workforce infiltration and pressures from Hezbollah-linked militant groups. Moreover, the Beirut-Montreal route would be the only air service directly linking Lebanon to North America. Within days the Americans' concerns rose to the highest levels in both Foreign Affairs and Transport. It was agreed that Canadian ministers do a special review of the matter.

The discussion that took place at the cabinet meeting at the end of May turned out to be deeply contentious. According to sources,[5] ministers were divided, some especially those with large numbers of Lebanese Canadians in their ridings, being strongly in favour of the new service, others being opposed. However, the primary opposition did not relate to the question of security itself but to the risk of offending the US administration. Deputy Prime Minister John Manley was chairing the meeting since Prime Minister Chrétien was attending a Canada-European Union summit in Athens. Manley underlined that proceeding with the flights would be construed, in his estimation, as open defiance of the US, which would certainly damage Canada-US relations. But given that there was no consensus in cabinet, he said he would contact Chrétien for his views. The prime minister's response was said to be quick and definitive. Air Canada's licence to operate the controversial flights was to be revoked.

The decision was not cost-free. Having already sold thousands of fares to eager customers, the airline had to compensate them. The advance costs in marketing the flights and establishing the flight infrastructure had been considerable. And several months later, in a move that was never made public, the federal government provided the airline with a multimillion-dollar settlement.

The atmosphere in the wake of the World Trade Centre attack was grim and oppressive. The strict security procedures that all of us must endure at airports today are the legacy of that time. But they are as nothing compared to the violations of personal liberties inflicted on several Canadian Muslims as part of a poorly targeted crackdown. Actions taken then represent a terrible stain on Canada's application of the rule of law.

The news that Canadian Maher Arar was detained on a return journey to Canada at an airport in New York quickly became public. His being spirited away by US authorities first to Jordan and then to Syria leaked out shortly thereafter. To me and many others, this move was strikingly arbitrary. It appeared to be a shocking violation of Arar's freedom. How could he have been detained without charge? By what legal authority was he transported to a third country? If he was suspected of something, why was he still not allowed to continue his journey home, under surveillance, where his suspect activities – if any – could have been appropriately investigated by police?

I had a good colleague and long-time friend who worked in the department on international security issues. When I raised these questions with him, his response was telling, and I think reflected the attitude of many working in Canada's security network at the time. "I understand your concern, but we don't know the evidence that the Americans have on him. And the Syrians are well placed to learn the truth." Such was the post-9/11 climate that even someone, who I thought would stand by due process and the rule of law, was acceding to assumptions about US investigatory prowess and condoning the use of torture. The injustice suffered by Arar was later well documented and the government awarded him $10 million in compensation due to the complicity of the RCMP and other Canadian authorities in his mistreatment.

His case was very much in my mind when I received an urgent call from the international relations manager of Air Transat, George Petsikas on January 5, 2006. Shortly after taking off from Montreal and entering US airspace on a flight to the resort city Zihuatanejo, Mexico, US fighter aircraft had been scrambled to accompany the Boeing 737 passenger jet in US airspace. Reviewing the passenger manifest which was automatically transmitted upon take-off, US authorities spotted a name on the American "no-fly" list. When I received Petsikas's call, the aircraft was over US territory, and Petsikas feared that it would be forced to land at a US airport. Instead the US patrol accompanied the flight through US airspace and allowed it to continue into Mexican skies. But on landing in Acapulco, the suspect passenger, Sami Kalil, and his family were detained by Mexican police.

With the flight still in mid-air over the US and immediately before alerting my chain of command in Foreign Affairs, I called a former colleague and friend from the parliamentary press gallery. A journalist for many years before joining the department, I was always circumspect in discussing my work with my former colleagues. If I spoke to reporters to provide background about departmental business, it would characteristically be with the knowledge of the department's media relations and relevant geographic or policy divisions.

But this time was different. My objective was to draw immediate public attention to the incident out of fear that without publicity, Kahil could be targeted, and through "extraordinary rendition," be taken to one of many US-sponsored black sites. My journalist colleague passed on what I told him, and shortly afterwards the story went public, through the news cooperative Canadian Press. It was reported that Kahil was being detained at the Acapulco airport, and his family was being returned to Canada via the same Air Transat aircraft they had arrived on. I contacted both the Mexico geographic desk and our embassy in Mexico directly to ensure that they were aware of Kahil's plight and that he would receive the consular assistance provided Canadians in difficulty abroad. My objective was to ensure that what had happened to Arar not happen to Kahil. As his wife, Rima was quoted as saying she was "terrified that the US air marshals would take him somewhere and he would disappear."[6]

Was there a reason Kahil was on the US no-fly list? Kahil had been denied refugee status in Canada in 1993 based on the immigration and refugee board's finding that he was connected to Hezbollah in Lebanon. Kahil denied being a Hezbollah member, pleading that he had always resisted efforts by Hezbollah to recruit him and had even been tortured for his refusal to cooperate. He was eventually accepted as a Canadian resident under the legal sponsorship of his Kuwaiti-born wife. He was a legitimate resident of Canada with no criminal record. My aim was that he not become a victim of the dark machine of extraordinary rendition that operated as part of the post-9/11 hysteria.

Fortunately, Kahil was returned to Canada on January 7 in a Canadian government plane, escorted by RCMP officers. The plane flew a circuitous flight path avoiding US airspace. As it turned out, Kahil later appealed to US authorities to have his name removed from the no-fly list, which he succeeded in doing by September 2006. They had accepted his innocence. When I spoke to Petsikas for this book, he remembers the incident clearly. He resents to this day that Air Transat was forced to hire a private plane to carry Kahil back to Canada at a cost of $30,000.

* * *

During my seven years in the trade services policy branch, we negotiated many agreements, winning significant new access to numerous markets: France, Brazil, the United Kingdom and the United States among them. But the negotiation that turned out to be most pertinent for my own career was the one with South Africa.

I was pleased in Spring 2003 that we received an invitation from South Africa to negotiate a new bilateral air agreement. I had followed closely for years the events in that country that for so long had maintained the formal policy of racial separation and discrimination known as *apartheid*. And I had exulted with so many when African National Congress (ANC) leader; Nelson Mandela was able to lead the negotiations to end the white supremacist regime and establish a new democratic polity. I was eager to see South Africa some 13 years into its democratic transition. Landing in Johannesburg and travelling by van to Pretoria only 50 kilometres to the north, I was immediately impressed by both the modernity of the country and its wonderfully open landscapes. Still, it was a revelation that the South Africa of townships and the poverty associated with many of them, can be virtually invisible to a casual traveller moving within the highly developed islands of South African wealth.

The negotiations turned out to be difficult to the point of stalemate. There was a clear interest on both sides in establishing direct air links between Toronto and Johannesburg, but the route posed technical difficulties both in terms of distance and altitude of the Johannesburg airport. Eager to develop the market, Air Canada sought the operation of routes through intermediate points with the ability to pick up new passengers (fifth freedoms). This the South Africans would not agree to, in the belief that this would divert traffic from South African Airways already serving these intermediate points. In the face of this resistance, we rolled back the Canadian request to "code-sharing", a system whereby an airline will sell seats on an allied airline already operating in the market. What was regrettable was that the South African lead negotiator was apparently perplexed by this offer and also appeared to have no flexibility other than to agree to direct flights.

We learned something about his background during a lunch we hosted at Canada's official residence in Pretoria. He told us he had spent many of the *apartheid* years in exile in Zambia, working for the ANC's underground military wing, Umkhonto we Sizwe, or Spear of the Nation. The organization was charged with infiltrating saboteurs into South Africa and assisting in fomenting militant resistance in the townships. We were unsure whether he felt uncomfortable in his now more conventional role, or whether he was being restrained by unseen and obstinate superiors.

Regardless, this round of negotiations failed, without even a hint of a possible way forward.

Little did I know that some five years later I would be given the opportunity to serve in the Canadian high commission in Pretoria. My visit there in 2003 allowed me to be more informed about the country than I would have been otherwise. When the assignment was offered, I was eager to take it on. In the meantime, however, my career was about to take a new turn, into the perennially tortuous bi-ways of trade policy's beleaguered outpost: softwood lumber.

In the years since, the adoption of Canada's "blue sky policy" in 2006, Canada has negotiated 22 agreements that offer unrestricted access to bilateral air traffic markets. Flights of any size can be operated to all destinations without any limit on frequency. Many of these have been reached with smaller countries, including many Caribbean states, and also include larger markets such as Brazil, South Korea and the European Union. Will this trend continue in the more contentious atmosphere of international trade relations that have followed the steady discrediting of globalization as exemplified by the Trump presidency and Brexit? Could air transport agreements become greater hostage to broader political and economic interests?

Aviation has operated to the side of the multilateral trading system yet provided customers and markets with services they need in the global economy. Perhaps it will continue to succeed on its own track. But the major challenge which was only beginning to be addressed when I worked in the field, is how a still-expanding airline industry can survive in the future, in an economy striving to reduce greenhouse gas emissions and arrive at a carbon-neutral future. Preserving air traffic rights as an element of the rules-based international system is not the only challenge negotiators of today and tomorrow face. Addressing the environmental impact of the aviation industry will be an as great, or greater challenge.

5

A Dickensian Deal (2007)

Canada has enormous forests that can produce an abundance of lumber, and there is a construction market in the United States to buy much of it. In normal conditions, this combination of plentiful supply and continuous demand should engender a vigorous market of willing sellers and ready buyers. Instead, the sale of softwood, or construction, lumber has been the sorry subject of a hopelessly byzantine dispute between Canada and the United States for some 40 years, with no prospect of an end in sight.

That it has lasted so long is principally the fault of a US lumber industry eager to secure its share of its domestic market at prices that will assure them ample returns. In an enduring achievement of expert lobbying, an industry-based largely in the US Pacific Northwest and the South has persuaded successive US administrations to swaddle it in a protective cover. This protectionism, in turn, has spawned on the Canadian side an administrative machine comprising governments and industry, not so much to oppose it but to manage the market limits imposed.

I remember the beginning of this longstanding dispute when first drawn to my attention in 1982 as a reporter with *The Calgary Herald*. Alberta along with all other lumber-producing provinces was hit with the first round of punitive US duties, in what turned out to be a seemingly eternal dispute. The issue followed me into my job in trade communications in Foreign Affairs. The drafting of news releases of lumber-related trade actions and counteractions always seemed to be a last-minute ritual of the Christmas season.

I finally had to confront the matter head-on when in January 2007, I was put in charge of the softwood lumber controls division. I had succeeded in a competition to replenish the Department's executive ranks. It had been a drawn-out process. A couple of years earlier, the Department announced that for the first time it was opening access to its executive cadre (directors and above) to employees who were not career foreign service officers. Traditionally career diplomats were recruited through regular foreign service competitions conducted nationwide. Success in these competitions opened the way to a career in the Department including the so-called "rotational" status under which officers would be eligible for postings as diplomats in Canadian embassies abroad.

But in 2005, through a rare, one-time-only competition, employees outside the official foreign service officer ranks, like myself, were offered an opening into a full diplomatic career. The process included written exams, executive aptitude tests including work simulations, and interviews before a board of three Departmental senior managers. I put my name forward in both the foreign service and international trade streams and to my great pleasure succeeded in both. It was truly fortunate for me in that no similar competitions have been held since. But following my success in the 2006 competition, my next step was to identify an upcoming vacancy in the Department's executive ranks and convince senior management that I could handle the job.

There was an open directorship in the yet-to-be-organized softwood lumber controls division to administer the just-negotiated Softwood Lumber Agreement, the fourth such deal between Canada and the United States. The eager victim of my own career ambition, I was assigned to be the director of softwood lumber controls under the 2006 Softwood Lumber Agreement.

The importance of forestry to Canadian trade is not what it once was when decades ago forestry products, including pulp and paper, constituted Canada's single largest export sector. Manufactured goods and energy products lead the way today. Still, forestry is an important industry and the government resources devoted to defending it are substantial. In my days in trade communications, I had overseen the department's involvement in the international forestry partnerships program, an initiative aimed at responding to potent criticism of Canadian forest management practices by environmental groups. These criticisms reached their height in the early '90s during the campaign against the logging of old-growth forests on Clayoquot Sound on the west coast of Vancouver Island. Protesters blocking logging roads leading into the forest captured international attention that led to threatened boycotts of Canadian lumber by several European countries. In response, the Canadian government brought together the provinces (who are responsible for the resource) and industry to defend this important export industry. But in creating the international forestry partnerships program, the aim of the members was not just to defend the image of the industry, but also to work towards the implementation of sustainable forestry practices that could withstand environmental scrutiny. According to a 1999 statement of the Council of Forest Ministers, the program aimed to make stakeholders "better stewards of the forest resource and help us be recognized as such . . . (and) assist the forest sector maintain its international competitive edge while creating jobs in the numerous . . . communities that depend on our forests."[1]

Our role in the department was to liaise with our missions in Europe to provide them with continuously updated information about the reality of the Canadian forest industry and the steady improvements in Canadian forestry practices. It was the missions' job to persuade European decision-makers that Canadian forests were being sustainably managed and dissuade them from imposition of lumber import restrictions. Through persistent efforts throughout the late '90s, Canadian embassies in Berlin, Brussels and London in particular were able to fend off an array of regulations meant to limit access to European markets of Canadian forest products supposedly harvested using environmentally unsustainable practices.

What was galling in the early 2000s about the efforts of the US softwood lumber coalition to impede Canadian lumber exports was that the Canadian industry and the provinces that oversaw it had taken extensive measures to create a more environmentally sustainable industry. Such improvements which required considerable investment should have in theory lowered Canada's vulnerability to charges of subsidizing its industry and inviting trade retaliation. Under joint government and industry initiatives, the regeneration of Canadian forest stands was brought into balance with the quantity of timber harvested. Although "stumpage fees," or royalties, charged companies for cutting timber varied from province to province, they were set by taking into account the amount of public investment in replanting forests, which task, if not mandated to industry, was undertaken by the provinces themselves. Nonetheless, the continuing complaint of the US industry was that the level of these royalties constituted a subsidy by Canada, and irrespective of the adjustments provinces made, the US industry would not relent in their charges of subsidization and dumping.

The finalization of the 2006 Softwood Lumber Agreement was negotiated by the Stephen Harper government elected in January of that year. The Agreement's predecessor had expired five years before, and the previous government had striven to strike down US countervailing and anti-dumping duties that had been imposed in the meantime. Appeals made to various panels of the NAFTA and the WTO had produced, from the federal government's perspective, a largely unblemished record of favourable rulings for Canada. The reviewing panels found little evidence of hidden government subsidies, nor a deliberate effort to sell lumber below prices prevailing in Canada's domestic markets – the key indicators for the imposition respectively of countervailing or anti-dumping duties. However, at every turn, the US industry and government devised new ways to appeal, delaying interminably the possibility that a final judgement at the WTO would ever definitively resolve the matter. As Elaine Feldman, a senior trade policy official now retired wrote in a study of the 2006 Agreement: "Litigation created an endless loop in which contradictory rulings were handed back and forth between NAFTA panels and the US International Trade Commission . . . (T)aking complaints to both the NAFTA and World Trade Organization . . . only further muddled the hoped-for outcome."[2] Shortly after arriving in office, Prime Minister Harper was eager to notch a success for his still fledgling minority government. The department's negotiators were advised to bring long-meandering softwood lumber talks to a close.

The deal resulted in the reimbursement of most of the duties paid by the Canadian companies over the several years when no agreement had been in place. The pay-out was some $4 billion worth, short of the $5.3 billion collected by US Customs, but enough, by improving their balance sheets, to satisfy the companies. However, the rules for the new regime were the most complex ever negotiated in the long-running dispute. Lumber exports to the US from Quebec, Ontario, Saskatchewan, and Manitoba would be subject to quantitative quotas, limiting the amount that could be sold to the US. In Alberta and British Columbia, there would be no hard quotas, but an export, or surge, tax imposed on any quantities that exceeded a certain amount. As the newly appointed director of the softwood controls division it would be my job to police the quotas and monitor the quantities subject to tax.

Often in the discussion of trade policy, observers talk about "free" versus "managed" trade. There is no better example of the latter than the Softwood Lumber Agreement of 2006. This was one very large anomaly in the era of ever-greater free trade among market economies and an especially glaring one in the tariff-free environment established by the FTA and the NAFTA.

My new office was in the former but newly renovated Ottawa city hall that was effectively becoming the department's trade annex. Before several Ottawa-area municipalities were amalgamated by the province in the late '90s, these local fiefdoms resisted what they suspected would be their imminent demise by building modern new headquarters. The city of Ottawa was no exception, commissioning renowned architect Moshe Safdie to design a neo-modernist extension to the existing '50s tower that sat on Green Island in the Rideau River. With the departure of the city administration, after the forced merger of all the Ottawa-area municipal governments, the building became vacant. Its location on the opposite bank of the Rideau from the Pearson Building made it the obvious choice for an expanding Foreign Affairs, and particularly for the department's trade branch. In homage to Japanese office design principles which were then the rage, managers occupied the core of each floor and were surrounded by cubicles for their staff that extended in concentric rows to exterior windows. My office was a small room with a four-person conference table into which exterior light struggled to penetrate a translucent glass wall. Outside my door laboured an array of export permit officers whose responsibility was to issue the licences for every lumber export destined to the United States.

In January 2007, I was introduced to the cumbersome ongoing administrative machinery that would make the softwood lumber agreement work. My division had the practical responsibility to manage the quotas and monitor the levels that would trigger surge taxes. There was a second division – called softwood lumber policy – whose role was to coordinate the regular multilevel consultations with the provinces and US trade authorities in both the department of commerce and the State department. Given the Agreement's many moving parts these consultations were virtually constant, involving in each instance a different group of players. At the top of the "governance" structure was the binational softwood lumber council, a body that brought together the most senior officials of both the United States and Canada to review the ongoing operations of the agreement and give future guidance.

It was a revelation to me, in attending the first of these councils held in Washington, to see the abundance of brainpower deployed in this cause. At a reception organized by Canada in the Canadian embassy, I was struck by the legions of lawyers in attendance, illustrative of the hefty financial stakes involved in managing softwood lumber trade. As much as one theoretically preferred "free" trade, there was lots of money to be made in "managed" trade. It is estimated that legal fees paid out in the various cases preceding the conclusion of the 2016 Agreement amounted to some $500 million![3] What's more, given the perennial nature of this dispute, it was evident that many of its parties, American and Canadian, might have an interest in maintaining quotas, export taxes or similar restrictive arrangements, to secure, and even inflate, their piece of the pie.

My boss, Suzanne McKellips, the director-general of Canada's export control bureau, likened the situation to the interminable lawsuit of Jarndyce and Jarndyce that is the foundation of the plot of Charles Dickens's *Bleak House*. The suit Dickens describes has deteriorated into nothing more than a struggle to extract professional fees from a case whose objective (the settling of an estate) has become entirely secondary. "It's about nothing but Costs, now. We are always appearing, and disappearing, and swearing, and interrogating, and filing, and cross-filing, and arguing, and sealing, and motioning, and referring, and reporting . . . and equitably waltzing ourselves off to dusty death, about Costs."[4]

Prospects for profiteering aside, the 2006 Softwood Lumber Agreement was not signed at an auspicious moment for the Canadian lumber industry. Housing construction in the US was in a steep downturn due to extensive mortgage defaults in various regional markets. These defaults were in fact the most important precursor of the 2008 world markets crash that summoned a precipitous contraction of economies worldwide. Canada's softwood lumber exports had been falling since 2004 from $11 billion and were still dropping when the Agreement was signed, eventually bottoming out at about $5.7 billion in 2009.

The quota system applied in Quebec, Ontario, Manitoba, and Saskatchewan. The quotas imposed on Canadian lumber companies were not fixed amounts, but annually adjustable quantities based on historic moving averages. The calculations followed extremely complicated equations, but recent declines in Canadian lumber sales were built into the calculation of future quotas, meaning that they were bound to diminish over the first few years of the Agreement. Moreover, a particularly perverse condition of the Agreement was that quotas would be reduced as market prices fell, so that companies would not only have to sell less by volume, but prices per thousand-board-feet would also be lowered.

The acute awareness of these falling indicators by Canadian lumber company executives stimulated some creative interpretations of the Agreement's mathematical quota calculations as a way to forestall, or reverse, the short-term trend. The calculations were doubly important since they would have an effect not only on the global quota level but also the share that each company would receive in what was a rapidly shrinking market. The management of this twisted thicket of quadratic functions and logarithms was the responsibility of the young senior economists that I had the good fortune to hire during my first weeks in the office.

The export, or surge, taxes, which applied to Alberta and British Columbia, posed another challenge. The thresholds lumber companies would have to hit before the taxes would apply were set for entire provinces and not for individual lumber companies. Similar to the quota system, the tax rate would rise punitively in a range from five to 15 per cent as market prices fell. As shipments would arrive at the border, the exporter would inform permit officers in my division of the quantities involved. But there was no coordination between lumber companies on total aggregate volumes, and no individual company could know whether their shipment had reached the threshold to trigger the surge tax. That level would be declared by the Canada Revenue Agency based on the numbers received from Canadian customs border posts daily.

In the Department, it was generally believed, in the interests of preserving harmony among all participants in the agreement, that surge tax thresholds ought to be avoided. At the same time, it was not considered the government's duty to advise individual companies to hold exports back. This led to the rather uncomfortable process of monitoring Alberta and British Columbia exports with the hope that the threshold would not be breached, but not being prepared to do anything to stop it. Nonetheless, if the taxes did kick in, we needed to be prepared for the negative fallout from the companies that would bear the brunt of the tax.

The daily working life of a softwood lumber bureaucrat is illustrative of the rather aggravating complexity of "managed trade" agreements and the rather unforgiving hours of trying to manage them. In spring 2007, several of my officers and I gathered at the art deco headquarters in Washington DC of the US Department of Commerce, named the Herbert Hoover Building after the president who was burdened with managing the initial years of the Great Depression. We were there to tackle some of the initial issues that had arisen to date. While most of our exchanges with US counterparts were generally civil, my direct equivalent, a commerce veteran with the somehow evocative – even Dickensian – name of Jim Terpstra, took pleasure in being obstinate and rhetorically irritating. He had been on the file for years, and it was difficult to determine whether his obstreperousness was for his and others' entertainment, or whether he genuinely sought tactically to extract some yet-to-be-determined advantage. Since his endgame seemed obscure, I assumed his demeanour was largely an act that we had to humour. Yet our meetings proceeded with difficulty as we sought to counter his rhetorical thrusts and dispose of his objections.

The most important issue during the meeting was the need to reconcile the statistics that we had on Canada's softwood lumber exports with those the US customs authority had in its possession. Given the need for Canadian companies to remain within their quotas or avoid surge tax thresholds, correct numbers were obviously vital for the success of the Agreement. My US counterpart was claiming Canadian companies had vastly exceeded the appropriate levels and warned that measures might need to be taken to punish non-compliance. What made his assertions so aggravating, was that the more he stormed on, the more time was being wasted before sitting down with the technicians in the US customs bureau to compare and reconcile our databases.

The meeting eventually closed with our commitment to work diligently to review the numbers, which is precisely what my staff had come to Washington to do. In prolonged talks, which took place in at least three separate sessions in both Washington and Ottawa – to reconcile only the statistics from the first quarter – we were able to bring our numbers within a four per cent difference which, given the complexity of the trade, was considered adequate reconciliation. But the person-hours expended to reach this decision were substantial.

The inefficiencies involved in maintaining such a system were obvious, although the direct cost to the Canadian taxpayer was limited. Expenses for operating the Softwood Lumber Agreement were offset by the revenue generated from the sale of export permits. But as economists point out, such expenditures constitute lost opportunity costs. Money expended for administrative purposes is money diverted from investment in more productive activity.

The minutiae of managing the agreement may foster a certain ennui, but enactment of the provisions can have a rather profound real-world effect. On the eve of the 2007 Canada Day long weekend, I was summoned to the office of international trade deputy minister Marie-Lucie Morin. The deputy's office was still located on the eighth floor of the Pearson building, so we marched in early summer heat across the Rideau River bridge separating the buildings for this relatively rare meeting with the department's top civil servant. Morin wanted to know whether figures from the end of June would reveal that Alberta and British Columbia had crashed through the threshold that would trigger surge taxes. Earlier in the month, McKellips had herself been asked to report to Morin about the likelihood of the threshold being broken. I had advised her on the strength of the figures that I had to date that, if the current trend continued, exports would fall short of the target. Unfortunately for me, further calculations made by my staff following her meeting suggested indeed that the export floor might be breached. Clearly, the fact that my initial data had caused McKellips to unintentionally mislead the deputy did not sit well with her. An economist by profession, she was a veteran of Canada's department of finance, and though normally friendly and courteous, she could also be justifiably exacting.

The stakes were high when I went to see Morin on the Friday afternoon of June 29. Making it particularly difficult to give the deputy a definitive answer was the fact that Saturday, June 30, would be a regular working day at the Canada-US border. For my staff and I, this was not going to be a celebratory Canada Day weekend. Rather, I assured the deputy that we would monitor closely the incoming data throughout the weekend to provide her with the latest on the morning of Tuesday, July 4 when everyone returned to work. I found among my analysts a volunteer to monitor the incoming permit applications, and through several calls a day he was able to keep me up to date. By Tuesday morning, I was pleased with the work that we had done but, given processing delays from freight-forwarders who frequently managed the permit applications for their customers, our numbers were still not definitive. We reported to McKellips that we were unable to say on the morning of July 4 whether the threshold had been breached, but it became evident in the following days that Alberta and British Columbia companies had "blown through" their surge tax thresholds. And this pattern would be repeated on numerous occasions in the following months adding new costs to the Canadian product and putting a further strain on access to the US market. For all the intense monitoring carried out on that Canada Day weekend, the results demonstrated the futility of a process that had no effect on companies' commercial behaviour and inevitably saddled them with higher costs. For everyone involved, from deputy minister Morin down, this "managed trade agreement" containing uncontrollable variables would be an ongoing administrative headache.

New annual quotas were to be negotiated for firms in the following years when part of the challenge was to re-allocate quantities following the closure of numerous Canadian mills that had become unviable. Major companies such as Abitibi Bowater, Domtar and Western Forest Products were forced to close several of their historic mills. Eventually, the outcome of the 2006 Agreement would be seen to represent a significant victory for the US industry's protectionist stance. Before the Agreement, Canadian companies commanded 35 per cent of the US market, against the US industry's 63 per cent market share. Post-agreement Canadian companies supply 28 per cent of the market relative to US firms' 71 percent.[5] In dollar terms, the softwood lumber market for Canadian producers recovered over time, but at $10.4 billion in exports in 2017, it had not returned to the $11-billion record of 2004. Softwood lumber is a sector that remains a vestige of what used to be seen as the mercantilist past. But protectionism has seen a strange and astonishing revival in the tariff wars characteristic of many trading partners' recent relations with the United States. Will zero-sum economic diplomacy set a new course for years to come, or will it constitute an aberration? Economists are beginning to contemplate an era where efforts to open markets and remove barriers will no longer be the default position for government policymakers. Instead, trade negotiations could again resemble the mercantilist jousting common before the mid-20th century establishment of the General Agreement of Trade and Tariffs. If ever there was hope that Canada-US softwood lumber trade would eventually be treated conventionally within a free trade arrangement, such a prospect seems inconceivable now. The Canadian lumber industry is once again labouring under new tariffs imposed by the US in 2017, which will lead in all likelihood to efforts to negotiate another restrictive agreement, and continued positive rulings in Canada's favour by WTO dispute panels mean little in the face of the United States' effort to disparage and emasculate that organization.

As much as I found my job as director of softwood controls interesting, my communications and policy background had not naturally prepared me for a role so dominated by mathematical calculation. Departmental management agreed that the position should preferably be undertaken by someone with an econometrics background. By mutual agreement, I negotiated a new post in another division that would permit me to manage an issue that, as shall be seen, would become – for a strange moment – more contentious than softwood lumber and significantly affect the outcome of the next federal election.

6

Trashing the Arts (2007–2009)

The colleague before me at my office conference table had worked for the Department for many years and a good many of them, as the officer responsible for managing grant applications from visual artists and museums. She was fuming. "You have lied to us. All the rumours are true. The program is being closed. You guys!" she raged in a sweeping accusation, referring to me and, vaguely, the rest of the department's decision-making hierarchy. She stormed out of my office. I understood her frustration. I had been doing my best not to lie, but frankly I had been disingenuous, offering fuzzy descriptions of the status of the international arts promotion program, or Promart.

When I accepted the job as director of the cumbersomely named public diplomacy and international cultural relations program, I was not aware that one of my duties would be to shut Promart down. I did know that the 2007 "strategic review" was underway, a government-mandated initiative to identify savings and eliminate activities that were not part of "core" services. However, I did not know, as I walked into my new office for the first time on that September morning, that the die had already been cast, that the decision had been made to sacrifice the program on the altar of what the deputy minister, Len Edwards, described as the "transformation agenda."

The Harper government was 18 months into power. It was determined in principle and by ideological inclination to cut government spending. What's more, it had a deep-seated suspicion of the Department, which it liked to characterize as a nest of superior elitists who turned their back on the rest of government in pursuit of an agenda that meant little to most Canadians. Even before Harper, such an attitude simmered in the core of the Privy Council Office and other government departments. But with the arrival of Harper, this trope became almost sanctified as doctrine. In an oft-repeated analogy, most Canadians took their coffee at Tim Hortons; the elites sipped their *lattes* at Starbucks. The government was with the Tim Hortons crowd, it claimed. Deputy Minister Edwards was acutely aware of this in his interactions with the so-called "centre" and he was determined to respond. The transformation agenda was his vehicle to bring the government around to a new way of seeing its foreign affairs department.

Having been on the ramparts of Canadian trade and foreign policy for several years and having come to identify with the value of the Department's mission, I found the disparaging attitude galling, not to say ignorant. Explaining Canada's role in the Gulf War and the Kosovo campaign; assembling the details of the NAFTA to help Canadians understand the most important commercial agreement Canada had ever signed; improving international flight connections between Canada and other countries, providing Canadian travellers more accessible international destinations; managing the complex arrangements of the Softwood Lumber Agreement in the interests of an important national industry that provided jobs across the country – these had been among my duties so far in my career, and I had carried them out believing them to be valuable for the department's clients and the public at large. There were few moments at my desk or in the field that I thought I was not trying to give taxpayers their money's worth.

Promart was a $4.7 million fund that had been put in place in the '70s. Its chief purpose was to raise Canada's profile internationally by showcasing abroad the work of Canadian musicians, writers, filmmakers and visual artists. As a 1975 cabinet memorandum stated, the fund was part of a program "to support effectively foreign policy objectives, taking fully into account Canada's domestic cultural policies; to promote abroad Canada's domestic, economic, social and political interests; to reflect internationally the growing creativity and scope of Canadian culture and to promote . . . the export of Canadian cultural manifestations, [and]; to improve professional opportunities abroad for Canadian artists . . ."[1]

In its 35-year history, there had been several attempts to ditch the program by governments of various stripes. As in 2007, the argument had always been made that issuing cultural grants was not strictly part of the department's core responsibilities. But this point of view was previously rejected on grounds that highlighting Canadian culture abroad was part of maintaining Canada's international image and its "brand." Moreover, the grants helped increase exports by Canada's cultural industries, which provided net benefits to the Canadian economy. However, this rationale was not adequate for the Harper Conservatives. They arrived in office proclaiming their scorn for "soft power" diplomacy. They did not see the value in seeking to influence foreign opinion leaders through public relations campaigns, or embellishing Canada's brand with wider international audiences. They wished a foreign policy that would focus on "hard" Canadian interests: protecting Canada's security, offering consular services to Canadians abroad, promoting trade and investment. Even the latter was seen as less than a priority when it came to cultural industries.

From my perspective, the new government had a far too narrow view, born of a lack of experience among the Conservative Party's leaders in international affairs and an associated lack of interest. In one of his year-end interviews following his first months in office, Harper admitted that he had been unaware of the demands the international agenda would put on him and his government. The need for a major evacuation of Canadians from crisis-prone Lebanon in the summer of 2006, involving a major logistical effort led by Foreign Affairs, had been a rude awakening for the Conservatives. But dealing with the foreground requirements of foreign policy was still a long way from adopting complex strategies to influence and engage with international opinion and further Canadian interests in a less tangible sense. So public diplomacy and cultural programming were sitting ducks.

The role that I would be asked to play became clear within the first few days of my taking over the public diplomacy and culture directorship. I reported to Renetta Siemens, director-general of the culture and education branch, and she asked me to prepare a treasury board submission to endorse and finalize a strategic review recommendation to close Promart. I was to understand that the recommendation was not yet a decision. But the treasury board submission would make the case, outlining of course the up- and down-sides of such an action. This would need to be done in secret, as the various clients, such as symphony orchestras, publishers, museums and filmmakers, which traditionally received the grants, must not know in advance of what treasury board ministers might decide. To preserve secrecy, it was calculated that we also needed to keep the news from the majority of employees in my division. So began months of calculated insincerity as we sought to deflect inquiries from stakeholders about the "rumours" that the program was destined for closure.

My personal inclinations regarding the value of cultural programming were irrelevant. I had heard the complaints from Conservative-leaning colleagues about attending concerts of Canadian orchestras in almost empty halls in some European capital, or the outrage from a ministerial staffer that Promart had funded a Canadian rock band called Holy Fuck at the UK's Glastonbury music festival (where it was applauded by audiences and acclaimed by critics). However, the Vancouver Symphony Orchestra was about to undertake a major concert tour of South Korea, Macau and China, including concerts in Beijing and Shanghai, where its brilliant director Bramwell Tovey would feature some original Canadian work by a Chinese-Canadian composer. The tour would turn out to be a tremendous success, giving Vancouver profile as a modern, dynamic multicultural city in advance of the 2010 Winter Olympics. In later assignments abroad in South Africa and Chile, I was also able to see how audiences embraced performances by Canadian classical and jazz musicians who had received some travel assistance from the embassy.

My personal preference would have been to keep the program. It was a relatively small program with tangible outcomes. But my duty as a civil servant was to give it its last rites. It was a test case for me not only in carrying out my non-partisan duties, but also in learning how to manage the dismantlement of an organization, which for any manager in the public or private sector is a valuable administrative skill.

Drafting a treasury board submission is one of those necessary but still rather esoteric tasks that helps drive the machinery of government. It is more than a process of accounting for the increased or – in this case – decreased expenditures. It requires a narrative justification; a tally of the jobs involved and a plan to manage the employees affected; a communications plan to explain the initiative; and a variety of other exacting minutiae. It must also receive the approval of the highest echelons of the department, including the minister, before it is submitted to the treasury board for approval.

Layered on top of this already complex matrix were a further series of more abstract exercises to be incorporated in the federal government's "performance management" process. There was a well-established trend in the private sector where management regimes sought to document business objectives and evaluate their success that went beyond strict financial balance sheets. In seeking to run government more like a business, as so many management theorists have advocated, the federal government adopted a new accountability system which went beyond the traditional structure of the budget, estimates and public accounts. The government, under the tutelage of the treasury board, devised a "management accountability framework" to guide the drafting of "reports on plans and priorities" (RPP) and "departmental performance reports" (DPR). As I prepared the treasury board submission to recommend the closure of Promart, I had also to prepare my division's contribution to the RPP and DPR. Parallel to this exercise, we needed to contribute to the department's "integrated business plan", which among other things would calculate how many "full-time equivalent" (FTE) positions (colloquially known as jobs) would be needed to carry out our functions. Without wading further into this acronym thicket, I was able to advise that preparing the RPP and the DPR consumed about 30 per cent of the time of my own "FTE", and a good portion of those of others. My pride in my work as a federal civil servant notwithstanding, I was not alone in believing these exercises to be of limited value. I would challenge anyone who is not a participant in this process to derive any useful information from copies of any department's RPP or DPR, which look to be little more than lists laid out in boxes. The need to feed the treasury board goat "generates a heavy workload in all government departments and agencies."[2] Donald Savoie, Canada's foremost theorist on government administration has likened "the public sector's version of how the private sector decides" as "speaking in tongues"[3] and "turning a crank that's not attached to anything."[4]

These bureaucratic burdens were at best distracting, when we had before us the very practical challenge of devising the Promart closure plan, major components of which were timing and communication. Many of the grants to arts organizations, including particularly symphony orchestras, were reviewed and approved well ahead of the events they were meant to fund. Organizations were applying in 2007 for events to take place in 2008 and 2009. It was clear that ending Promart at the beginning of the fiscal year (April 2008 to March 2009) would mean that we needed to inform organizations now that they would receive no funds the following year. This was sure to confirm suspicions that the program was ending. As much as this might seem the right thing to do, the official decision had not been made, and there was the chance that some ministers on treasury board may have other ideas. Therefore, director general Siemens and assistant deputy minister Drew Fagan were successful in convincing deputy minister Edwards that the way past this conundrum was to phase out the program over the next two years. This would allow us to offer some of our traditional clients the assistance that they had historically come to expect without prematurely signalling the demise of the program. The treasury board submission would therefore ask for a grants budget of $3.9 million for the next two fiscal years before Promart was finally terminated.

The submission did not sail through entirely unopposed. International Trade Minister David Emerson saw value in the program to support larger trade missions with a sophisticated public diplomacy element. However, his concern was placated by a promise to draw up – after the cut – a joint Heritage Canada and Foreign Affairs policy team to conceptualize an alternative program. (I was later part of this team whose efforts came to naught in the face of a complete absence of support from Emerson's cabinet colleagues and Emerson's waning influence given his political weakness as a Liberal-to-Conservative turncoat who was unpopular in his Vancouver riding.) The submission was approved, and the plans were – we thought – to be incorporated into the coming federal budget.

Finance Minister Jim Flaherty presented the budget on February 26, 2008. Nothing in his budget speech, nor in the accompanying budget documents made mention of the cut of Promart, or of another associated cultural program, Trade Routes, at Heritage Canada, nor could one find any reference in the copious budget estimates that were released several days later. Mystified, we communicated with treasury board and officials in the department of finance to determine whether the phase-out and closure were still on. We were advised, in no uncertain terms, that they were.

I admit to being shocked by this failure to outline the decision in the budget documents. As a journalist, I had spent many hours poring over budgets in years past believing them to contain the comprehensive story of governments' tax and spending plans. I had faith in the probity and transparency of the budget-making process. While knowing full well that governments often hide some of their decisions in the fine print, it had been my experience that the requisite information could always be found – somewhere in an obscure column or even footnote in the estimates – estimates upon which Parliament must vote and grant the sitting government its spending authority. In this case, the Promart decision and associated numbers were completely hidden from view. I spent hours scrutinizing the papers and sought help from colleagues in the department's budget planning directorate. There was nothing.

The strategic review was theoretically a "revenue-neutral" exercise. That meant that any cut in programs and operations had to show up as additions to others. At first, this neutrality was to operate within departmental branches, so that the funds from the Promart cut would show up elsewhere in the policy planning bureau. Eventually, I was shown a spreadsheet (although I was not left a copy) that showed the Promart funds had been added to the international organizations (funding for the UN, for example) and disarmament budgets, neither of which was part of the policy planning bureau's envelope. No one filing an access-to-information request would have been able to follow where Promart funds went. A political judgement had been made to scorn the fiduciary principles of the budget process and keep the public in the dark.

I could not keep my staff in the dark, however. They needed to know how much the grants budget had been cut, how we were going to manage the reduced funds, and how we were going to "manage our clients' expectations" (this latter is a favourite phrase of federal bureaucrats when talking about delivering bad news). I summoned the officers to the divisional conference room and informed them of what only I, my boss Renetta and one other employee had known with certainty during the previous several months. The 35-year cultural program, which they had faithfully administered, was going to be phased out over two years, and their jobs would be gone.

The fury of the visual arts officer was completely understandable. She and her colleagues had been told that there would be no official decision on the fate of Promart until the budget. Which was true, but insincere.

Tempted as I was to take each of the officers into my confidence and explain the real situation, I had valued my pledge to my director-general, assistant deputy minister and, by extension, the deputy minister to remain silent pending (what was expected to be) the budget announcement. In addition to managing the grants phase-out, I was charged also with managing the transition of my staff to new positions or, where possible and desired, to retirement.

Trouble was brewing in public. Although the possible reduction of cultural funding made few waves beyond arts organizations in English Canada, it became a *cause célèbre* in Quebec. Earlier culture program cuts had stirred criticism; the opinion-forming newspaper *Le Devoir* stirred fears about reduced arts funding on its front page, and a wickedly satirical YouTube video on the subject was going viral.[5] In it, Quebec folk singer Michel Rivard, previously of the popular group Beau Dommage, played himself seeking a grant from a committee of federal bureaucrats. Three too-obviously anglophone officials in grey were becoming agitated over Rivard's reference to "phoque," a seal featured in one of his best-known songs, confusing the word with the common English expletive. A fourth official, who has so mastered a Quebec *joual* accent that he thinks he can aid communication by simply being authentic, nonetheless appears to have little interest in the substance at hand. When Rivard tries to give some "pe*tites*" clarifications, the grey anglophones mishearing a reference to a woman's breasts, become completely flustered, and the chair stamps "rejected" on the application form.

The officers in my division were all fluently bilingual and had a deep knowledge of their artistic disciplines and of the arts communities in both English and French Canada. So, the portrait of the personalities on the fictitious approval board was utterly false. Nonetheless, the video presented an image of the Ottawa bureaucracy and its governing politicians that is an easy but unfortunate cliché for sections of the public, including in Quebec where federal bilingualism is often seen as having been far from successful. For Quebecers, for whom the encouragement of francophone culture remains a high priority, the overall impression conveyed by the video contained a kind of symbolic truth.

From February until August, we continued to operate Promart without any reference to phase-out and closure. Despite the uncertainty hanging over their futures, officers continued to discuss funding projects with our usual clients. I was impressed by their discretion and their loyalty in not revealing the true state of affairs. Yet the announcement would have to be made shortly before it became evident the money was running out. I was asked to draft a communications plan which would explain the phase-out, provide a clear rationale and prepare defensive lines for the inevitable criticism. That plan was never put into action.

On the evening of August 7, 2008, we learned that an unnamed source in the prime minister's office (PMO) had stated to several parliament hill reporters that Promart was being axed. The source cited three examples of the kind of grants that would no longer see the light of day: a $550 grant to present a filmmaker's *Confessions of a Drag Queen*; a $990 grant to present the film *Peking Turkey* to a London, UK, gay and lesbian festival; and a travel grant for Canadian journalist Gwynne Dyer and former Supreme Court judge Michel Bastarache to travel to Cuba to give speeches on Canadian foreign policy. The examples were selected in an obvious effort to trivialize the program and stir contempt among many of the government's more right-wing supporters. Wasteful and immoral arts programming was seen as a perfect wedge issue to rile up emotions and drive opinion in the government's favour. Sharply different perspectives between English Canada and Quebec did not seem to figure in the calculation.

A key flaw in the deliberate PMO leak was, none of the three examples had anything to do with Promart. They seemed to have been taken from some list of grants of unknown provenance that had been collated with the calculated aim of casting the dimmest light possible on federal cultural programming. We never knew the identity of the PMO source. But the prime minister's chief of staff at the time was Guy Giorno and his director of communications was Kory Teneycke, each known for a belligerent, take-no-prisoners approach to political communications.

We had always planned as part of a more traditional communications strategy that I would call Promart's historic clients to advise them individually of the closure of the program. Unfortunately, under the twisted-knife approach of the PMO, there could be no measured outreach schedule. I was put in the position on Friday, August 8 to call as many clients as I could to provide at least the courtesy of telling them our longstanding relationship was about to be severed. Of course, it did not help that I, as director of the program, had a personal scheduling conflict that the PMO would not have known or cared the least about. Suzanne and I had been married earlier that summer on June 14. We had delayed our honeymoon to start on August 9 to correspond with the date of the wedding of my cousin's son in Liverpool, England. Committed to my work though I was, I was not going to cancel this holiday. I made as many calls as I could that Friday before handing the remainder off to one of my deputies, John Bonar, to complete in the coming days. These were not easy conversations, but for the most part, the reaction was a wearied resignation. Most clients, despite our recent efforts to maintain business as usual, had believed the rumours of imminent closure were true.

It was a relief in the months to come to be able to find suitable new berths for the Promart officers. Through reassignment in the government; a couple of retirements; and transfers to the surviving core of the public diplomacy section, none of the officers encountered grievous hardship. Of course, for the officers, having provided exemplary service in an interesting and specialized field for many years, their morale took a hit.

The more damaging consequences for the Promart closure fell on the Harper government itself. The minority Conservative government held 10 seats in Quebec, which it had won with the support of about 20.7 per cent of Quebec voters. In regular political polling, the Conservatives were registering 30 per cent or higher in the summer of 2008,[6] suggesting the party could improve its standing in Quebec in an election expected soon. In polls immediately after the Promart cut, Quebec support fell below 20 per cent. And in the October 14, 2008 election, the Conservatives were held again to 10 Quebec seats with 21.7 per cent of the vote. It was widely acknowledged among political observers at the time, that had Harper not reduced the culture budget, he might have won a majority. For that, he had to wait another three years. A non-partisan civil servant or not, given the plainly deceptive game our political masters had played, I could not help but feel a certain poetic justice had been rendered.

It would take 18 months to wind Promart down. I had done my duty as a civil servant to lay out its final trajectory and had learned some management lessons. I was relieved that we had been able to help the staff find their feet either in retirement or new jobs. I was suffering neither guilt nor regret when I viewed the Department's list for vacant assignments abroad and saw the job of the political counsellor to the Canadian high commission in Pretoria was available. It was time to get out into the field. After having made the pitch for the job and being accepted, what followed were several months of briefings organized by the geographic desk and a steady stream of readings on the history and politics of South Africa. I was more than ready for this new assignment. I'd spent years working for the Department at headquarters. Now I would find out what it was like to work for Canada abroad.

7

The Unfortunately Named ... (2009)

We left Canada's late summer light 36 hours before and were now descending into the bright spring sunshine of the sprawling city of Johannesburg. My expectations for my first foreign-based assignment were high. I was eager to tackle this new role as political counsellor reporting to Canada's high commissioner (ambassador) to South Africa. My wife, Suzanne, and I were greeted in the modern airport lobby by the high commission's first secretary, the smiling and affable Marc Labrom, who would be my indispensable deputy over the next year. After being dropped briefly at our mission-owned house in Waterkloof Ridge, a suburb of South Africa's administrative capital Pretoria, I decided to make an initial call at the office, the Canadian High Commission (Canada's embassies to Commonwealth countries are referred to as high commissions). I arrived to learn that Dawie Jacobs, director of the Canada desk of the South African foreign ministry (DIRCO, Department of International Relations and Cooperation), wanted to speak to me urgently.

During our 30-minute drive from the Johannesburg airport to Pretoria, Marc had mentioned a story that had broken overnight concerning a white South African by the name of Brandon Huntley who had been granted refugee status by a Canadian Immigration and Refugee Board (IRB) judge. The favourable ruling was based on a claim of persecution of white South Africans by members of the black majority population. The story was in all major news outlets, giving Canada a suddenly higher profile than usual in what is the very active South African media.

So, the reason for Jacobs's call was not to welcome me on arrival. The refugee board decision had impugned South Africa's reputation as a world champion of racial equality. The fact that he wanted a meeting right away underlined the issue's importance for the South African government.

Diplomacy has esoteric rules. High Commissioner Adele Dion had herself only just arrived in the country a couple of days before. She had not yet been received by the foreign office to officially present her credentials – which meant that she could not yet have formal meetings with the South African authorities. As newly appointed political counsellor, I was second-in-command by default, thus chargé d'affaires, and therefore the designated hitter pending Dion's presentation of credentials. It was startling that on my very first day in a completely new assignment, I was being "called in" to receive what would inevitably be a scolding over Canada's supposedly insulting behaviour.

The basis of Huntley's claim was that white South Africans lived in danger of attack by black South Africans; that there was a prevailing climate of persecution based on racial hatred and bigotry; and that this alleged danger justified his claim for asylum as a political refugee. Huntley had arrived in Canada on a temporary work visa to work as a carney on the Canadian summer fairs circuit. But after two summers in Canada, he decided he no longer wanted to go back to his violence-prone homeland.

The reaction of the South African government to the Huntley case could not have come faster or been more indignant. In the government's view, the post-apartheid "Rainbow Nation" was the antithesis of a racist state. In the South African government's view, people of all races in South Africa live as equals, free from prejudice based on their skin colour. The principle was recognized in the South African constitution and was being adhered to in practice. Therefore, the decision of a Canadian judge had to be ill-founded and unacceptable.

The office where I was to meet Jacobs was only a few short blocks away. In late 2009, the South African foreign ministry was scattered in a variety of offices around the city. (It was shortly to move into a new and spectacular modern headquarters). Marc and I left through the security gate of the high commission and walked through streets covered by the red dust that typically accumulates before the seasonal spring rains. We were met at the designated DIRCO office and brought to a conference room where we encountered a roomful of officials, led by South Africa's State legal adviser, Sandea de Wet.

DIRCO had retained much of its experienced diplomatic talent following the transition to non-racial democracy, which meant, by force of circumstance, that most of my "accusers" were white. De Wet had extensive experience in international law. Jacobs had been among a group of white reformers in the late apartheid era.[1]

The official upbraiding began immediately, delivered in that impeccable diction perfected by both Afrikaner and English-speaking professionals in South Africa. That DIRCO's top legal official was in charge of this meeting underlined the gravity with which South Africa considered the "white refugee" case.

The South African government was deeply offended, said de Wet, that Canada would have given any credibility to charges of racism against South Africa. The ruling was a "serious assault on the South African government's integrity . . . We want there to be no misunderstanding of the seriousness of the matter."

It was utterly false to suggest, she said, that South Africa was not devoted to racial equality. It is entrenched in the democratic constitution and practised every day in social and business settings throughout the country. There were absolutely no grounds for a finding of racial discrimination. The IRB's findings were "untrue, untested, and unacceptable." South Africa was appalled that Canada, so supportive of the historic struggle against apartheid, could now be responsible for casting such a false aspersion against its longstanding friend in the international arena. Canada's relationship with South Africa was "solid and cordial", and Canada should "set the record straight" without delay.

In the minutes before the meeting, Marc and I had discussed with headquarters in Ottawa the position I would take. "Thank you," I said, "for bringing your concerns to our attention. Your position is clear. You have made it forcefully, and I understand it. Canadians recognize South Africa's considerable achievements in building a tolerant, multi-racial society."

As I spoke, I was acutely conscious of the irony that my chief interlocutors were white. These very comfortable government officials were not being disadvantaged by racial discrimination. Claimant Huntley's portrait of the sorry plight of whites in South Africa did not ring true in this room.

"I must point out that the Immigration and Refugee Board's decision is independent of the Government of Canada's point of view. The IRB operates at arm's length from the government and is not susceptible to outside influence.

"However, we will convey your views to our capital, and we can assure you that what you have said to us today will be brought to the attention of the Canadian Minister of Citizenship and Immigration."

I did not make specific reference to the minister's ability to seek leave to appeal IRB decisions to the Federal Court of Canada. To do so, would raise hope that the then-minister, Jason Kenney, would do so. I was certainly unaware at this stage of Kenney's disposition. But I did stress to the director that I would get back to her on our government's reaction to the message she had just so firmly delivered.

In fact, Kenney's response was quick. Within 48 hours, he announced that he would indeed seek leave to appeal the ruling to the Federal Court, based essentially on what his department described as the poor quality of evidence on which the IRB decision had been made. This was hardly sufficient to quell South Africa's ire. But it was the first step available to resolve the issue. And when I contacted DIRCO as promised, they were satisfied that a path had been opened to overturning the objectionable finding.

Thumbing through the newspapers at home at the end of my first week in Pretoria, a column on the Huntley case in the Johannesburg Star caught my eye. The columnist noted that the South African government had officially protested by calling in the Canadian High Commission's *chargé*, who was "the unfortunately named Mr. White."

Race relations constitute the unavoidable and obsessional theme that dominates so much of South African life. It is particularly potent when it comes to reflecting upon the high levels of violence that characterize South African society.

Our house sat at the edge of one of Pretoria's poshest neighbourhoods. Like all houses in the neighbourhood, it was surrounded by a tall and solid wall topped with coils of barbed wire and electric fencing. Entry was obtained through remote-controlled iron gates. The doors and windows were covered by steel grates. Within the house the sleeping area was separated from the other living areas by a heavy iron door, and once inside this "safe haven" the rest of the home outward to the exterior walls was protected by an alarm system.

Being at the edge of Waterkloof Ridge, rather than in the heart of the neighbourhood, meant that we were closer to some of South Africa's more quotidian realities. The house looked over a traffic circle beyond which there were open fields and in the distance a view of the Waterkloof military air base. Blue-coveralled casual workers would gather on the circle every day in hope that a local contractor would need their labour.

The weekend of our arrival, our gardener, who lived in separate quarters on our lot, called us to explain that his son had lost his life in a highway accident while fleeing police. We learned a few weeks later of a murder of a neighbour several doors away on Orion Avenue. The 90-year-old Hans Swemmer was a man I had seen at the local petrol station. A veteran of the Korean War, he had been killed in his home, and his white Mercedes stolen. Later in our stay, an Asian diplomat, living even closer to us than Swemmer, was involved in an armed shoot-out with robbers in his driveway when returning from Johannesburg's Oliver Tambo Airport.

During 2011 and 2012, on four separate occasions, the copper wiring carrying neighbourhood electricity was stolen from pylons outside our home. On each occasion the power failed, an extremely loud siren alarm was triggered, and our on-site diesel generator automatically kicked into action. One mid-summer day, firefighters were called to put out a fire lit by itinerants sleeping rough in an abandoned lot behind our house. A large, apparently luxurious manor immediately beside us was vacated shortly after our arrival and was soon occupied by squatters. Police arrived one day to investigate the death of an infant child. One night someone from the squatters' villa tried to climb our electric fence, once again setting off our alarm. After each alarm, an armed, Kevlar-vested officer from a private firm under contract to the high commission would arrive on the scene, and we would have to report, carefully through the grates in our windows that we were safe. We didn't need to look far to find violence and menace in South Africa.

South Africa continuously collects, analyses and makes public its crime rates. The government recognizes that crime is a dark blemish on their society, but progress on addressing it is slow. Although recent statistics show common assaults and robberies are in decline, murders, attempted murders, house robberies and car-jackings rose between 2015–16 and 2016–17.[2] Car-jackings were the highest in ten years (16,717); there were 19,016 murders, or 34.1 per 100,000 population, up from 18,673 the previous year (by comparison, Canada's 2017 murder rate was 1.8 per 100,000). In 2018, the number of murders in South Africa was among the highest in the world, outstripped only by Jamaica, El Salvador, Honduras and Venezuela.

The legacy of apartheid runs deep. It persists most obviously in South Africa's urban geography. The townships in which the black populations were isolated by law, remain for the most part the neighbourhoods where blacks live today. Unemployed men from Mamelodi and Atteridgeville, to Pretoria's northeast and northwest respectively, lack skills and education. They were allowed only the most basic education in the apartheid years. There are few available jobs for them to give them viable means of support. Hawking cheap goods at intersections is often the best they can strive for. They constitute an unsatisfied labour pool and a breeding ground of resentment and disdain.

But victims of crime are everywhere, not only in the wealthy suburbs, where a large portion of whites live. In fact, most crime takes place within black communities. In sheer numbers, blacks represent the majority of South Africa's crime victims. Still, many well-publicized crimes have potent racial characteristics. For example, the white supremacist Eugene Terre'Blanche was murdered by his two black farmworkers in 2010. In the same year, Bees Roux, a white rugby star, murdered a black police sergeant who was trying to take him into custody for drunk driving. And these contribute to a sense that crime reinforces the potent dividing line between the black and white populations.

Fraught relations between blacks and whites can manifest themselves readily in daily life. A generous and genteel Afrikaner neighbour agreed to lend us her piano for the duration of our four-year stay. The piano arrived in the bed of a *bakkie*, a pick-up truck, driven by a sturdy Afrikaner. He was accompanied by a blind piano tuner and, sitting on his haunches in the cargo bed, a black man of perhaps 25 or 30 with a much-weathered look. The Afrikaner and the helper manoeuvred the piano up some steps to the patio, from where it would be lifted into the adjacent living room. The Afrikaner entered first, carrying the piano over the lip of the door, the barefoot helper needed to step forward to balance himself, putting a foot briefly on the living room floor. A sharp look from his boss caused him to recoil immediately. It was evident that he was not allowed to even put one foot within the house. He stood shamefully back as the piano was finally pushed into place and tuned. As the tuning went on, the Afrikaner took the time to offer me his opinions about the debased condition of South Africa under the new multiracial regime. He averred that under God's will and according to prophesy, the country would be soon rescued by Germans coming from the sky!

Not all white South Africans enjoy wealth and status inherited from the days of apartheid. I was surprised when the first beggars I saw in Pretoria were a young white couple crouching at the side of a highway off-ramp into the heart of the city. A young white man begging for coins was a steady fixture at the intersection of our road with the main highway to Johannesburg. Publicity always surrounded President Jacob Zuma's occasional visits to white "informal settlements," or squatter camps, part of his effort to recognize that all was not well for all members of South Africa's white population. Brandon Huntley was a case in point. He was unemployed before deciding to leave South Africa on a temporary permit to work the Canadian summer fairs season.

Huntley's case need not have become public. If he had not asked his lawyer Russell Kaplan, himself of South African origin, to announce the result to Canadian media, the case might still stand as an IRB precedent. The decision might have been overlooked among the hundreds of cases that IRB panels decide every year and gone unchallenged. But Huntley was intent not only on winning refugee status but also on drawing attention to conditions, as he saw them, of white South Africans in general and establishing a precedent for future claims. He wanted it known that Canadian authorities recognized the perilous conditions experienced by white South Africans. Unfortunately for him, the evidence presented before the IRB was not as convincing to Minister Kenney, or the higher court, as it had been to the IRB judge.

Huntley claimed he was attacked by black men on half a dozen occasions, but never reported these assaults to police. There was no official, documented record. To bolster the case, his lawyer Kaplan presented his own sister, Lara Ann, as a key witness. Both siblings had been horrified by the violent assault on their brother during a home invasion. And Lara spoke of having been on two occasions "accosted by black South Africans and threatened with a gun."[3] Her experiences contributed to her assessment that black South Africans "believe that all whites are equally responsible for apartheid and that 'we should be eradicated and stomped on like an ant.'"[4] She went on to offer the opinion that "in any other country, a mass genocide . . . on such scale as is occurring against whites in South Africa, would be considered genocide and crimes against humanity."[5]

The testimony was emotional and opinionated, and no doubt sincerely expressed. But it did not sway federal judges. The Federal Court granted Minister Kenney's application for judicial review and the Federal Court of Appeal found that the case should go back to a newly constituted IRB panel. Ultimately at the end of a long legal process, a judgement by Federal Court Judge James Russell prevailed. There was "no objective evidentiary foundation" to claims of systemic discrimination.[6] He was dismissive of Huntley's claims to persecution. "There is no objective foundation for a finding . . . that he left South Africa because he fears race-based crime. He finds the lack of economic opportunities intolerable and he is looking for a better way of life. He is also, perhaps, fearful of the prevalent crime that exists in South Africa, but this is not, in my view, a sufficient objective basis to support a claim for persecution."[7]

The judge then went on to dismiss the argument that the Minister would never have sought leave to appeal without diplomatic pressure, and the original ruling favouring Huntley would therefore have stood. "Even if diplomatic pressure caused the government of Canada to inquire into the Decision, there is no evidence that the Minister brought the application for any reason other than that . . . he decided to seek judicial review because of . . . errors in the Decision itself." [8]

Huntley, after taking the case to the Federal Court of Appeal which ordered a new refugee determination case; subsequently losing on that second go-round; and finally losing an appeal of that decision, completed his odyssey through the Canadian courts. Huntley's lawyer, Kaplan, does not believe that Canadian courts have properly come to grips with the issue. "The victims of crime are not just victims of crime but rather victims of crime related to a Geneva Convention motivation, namely race, which makes them refugees."[9] However, as of June 17, 2014, his client Huntley had run out of options and was unprotected from deportation.

Other Canadian tribunals have weighed in on "white" persecution claims. Judge Alain Bissonnette, chair of an IRB Refugee Appeal Division, wrote the following in the case of six members of a white South African family seeking refugee status:

> South Africa remains a democratic society in which ethnic and political groups may express themselves and in which legal institutions pay equal heed to those in the black population as to those in the white population . . . Whereas . . . violence and crime do form an integral part of the reality experienced by citizens of South Africa, I am of the opinion that . . . the recourse [is] provided by the laws and the Constitution allow[s] citizens, lawyers and judges to identify those responsible, to combat impunity and to reaffirm the primacy of each person's fundamental rights.[10]

The jurisprudence in Canadian cases has now been so amassed that Huntley's lawyer, Russell Kaplan, says that "my honest belief is that decisionmakers are afraid to rule on racial grounds."[11]

During my posting in South Africa, many white citizens I met looked to me to validate their feelings of anxiety about living in their country. I didn't dismiss their fears. Yet the burden of crime is also borne by blacks in the crowded townships and informal settlements. The dangers of crime afflict everyone across the racial spectrum. As the Canadian judges concluded, general exposure to crime and violence does not represent racial discrimination.

In 2009, the South African government was right to raise the alarm over the original Huntley ruling. By doing so they set in motion a legal process in Canada that resulted in jurisprudence that quashed the claim that South African whites are targets of racial persecution.

South Africa is a fascinating country in historical and geopolitical terms. Its modern economy makes it a leader in Africa, and optimistic assessments see South Africa being at the vanguard of an economic transformation of the continent. Yet the country's still failing struggle to provide opportunity to its large population of disadvantaged black citizens, a legacy of apartheid, represents a huge impediment to its economic prospects. It also provokes internal political strain that influences its foreign relations. Its economic and political struggles had important implications for Canada's relations with South Africa and our ability to maintain a mutually advantageous partnership. During the years in which I was posted in South Africa, that partnership was strained in ways that went far beyond the row about the Huntley case.

8

Disillusioned Friends (2009–2012)

You didn't have far to look in 2009 to find optimistic forecasts about the future of Africa. Despite still assessing the impact of the 2008 financial crisis and recession, economists pointed out that African countries were outstripping much of the world in economic growth. The emerging narrative was that of a continent turning the corner from chronic under-development to vigorous expansion. In South Africa, the Brenthurst Foundation, the think tank established with the extraordinary diamond- and gold-derived wealth of the Oppenheimer family, proclaimed a new era of African prosperity. The foundation's director Greg Mills had just published *Africa's Third Liberation: The New Search for Prosperity and Jobs* which noted rates of growth of five per cent and more throughout much of the continent. He argued that the future lay not in more aid but in unlocking the potential for growth and trade.

This view dovetailed well with the Canadian government's evolving stance. International assistance was being focused on the neediest of African countries, while a push for greater investment and trade characterized our relations with the rest. This indeed fit with the international consensus on globalization, which was that of unleashing economic growth and – in the wake of greater prosperity – a perceived appetite among emerging middle classes for better governance.

This was the prevailing view at headquarters when I started my assignment in South Africa. It was a break from a past when Africa was viewed predominantly as deeply in need of Canadian initiatives in foreign aid. There was talk of the Department developing a new Africa strategy that would over-ride that view and bring a greater geopolitical and commercial focus to relations with African countries. In the meantime, pending articulation of such a strategy (which never came), our marching orders were to focus on economic opportunity and political cooperation to strengthen rule of law and democratic institutions.

The irony in this context was that South Africa, the continent's most developed economy, was lagging behind many of its less developed neighbours on the strict measure of GDP growth. Although its economy was larger than all others except for much more populous Nigeria, it was not rebounding from the recession, and South African business and foreign investors were losing confidence in the government's ability to re-ignite growth. A rapidly expanding economy was vital for South Africa as about 25 per cent of its workforce, for the most part black, was unemployed. The seemingly intractable problem of how to accelerate growth sufficiently to crack the back of crippling unemployment cast a long shadow on President Jacob Zuma's African National Congress (ANC) government.

I met President Jacob Zuma after his speech closing the South African Parliament's budget debate in February 2011. As is the custom, many ambassadors and other embassy staff decamped from Pretoria to Cape Town for Parliament's marquee proceedings during the southern summer political season. There was always the possibility of scoring "face time" with Zuma to press our concerns. I managed to get close to him as he circulated in the reception hall and stepped forward to introduce myself. I first complimented him on the budget's continued restraints on expenditure. Sound fiscal management had been one of the government's key objectives since the end of apartheid and had contributed to international confidence in South Africa's economy, especially during the years of growth in the early 2000s. Focusing on my specific brief that day, I raised the difficulty that Canada was having in convincing the South African government to finalize a nuclear cooperation agreement, the principal negotiations for which had been wrapped up a couple of years before. Zuma's round face was impassive; his dark eyes, slightly hooded, evinced no reaction, either to the compliment or the plea. He nodded silently and then moved on.

Zuma had just begun his first five-year presidential term. He was elected in June 2009 after already serving several months in office after ousting his predecessor, Thabo Mbeki. The Canadian government's assessment of Zuma's ascension was not positive. He was mired in corruption allegations over his role in a multi-billion-dollar purchase of military equipment.[1] Charges were put on hold through the manipulation, intimidation and replacement of senior justice officials. He had recently been acquitted of a rape charge[2] and, in a separate scandal, was about to pay a former ANC comrade and football club owner compensation for impregnating his teenage daughter.[3] His supporters in the ANC, in addition to the strong Zulu community to which he belonged, included many who sought to benefit from government appointments and contracts at all levels. Patronage was tacitly justified as reward due to the victors in the struggle against apartheid. So, in the eyes of many, "the ANC *was* a liberation organization and *is now* a benefits club."[4] All of the above led to a dim view of Zuma and the growing opinion that South Africa, rather than being the hopeful beacon for democracy in Africa, was starting to look like other shaky sub-Saharan African states.

I was not ready to endorse that view. Nelson Mandela famously wrote that South Africans had followed a "long walk to freedom." The final phase of that struggle started in 1976 with student protests in Soweto and expanded to a much broader civil resistance across the entire country that the ANC described as "the people's war." The apartheid government surrendered, and the first multi-racial elections brought the ANC and Mandela to power in 1994. South Africa's "new dispensation" was a milestone on the road to greater freedom worldwide. Fifteen years following the founding of the "Rainbow Nation," I was not prepared, arriving in South Africa as the high commission's political counsellor, to dishonour that legacy and be too quick to adopt a disillusioned view.

This perspective sustained me throughout my assignment and helped me and the two high commissioners I served to persevere when it became clear that South Africa's politics and economy were struggling to stay on track.

Despite Canada's officially friendly relations with South Africa and our declared hopes for its future, the relations between our countries had not recently prospered. Canada and South Africa increasingly found each other on opposite sides of debates in international fora. Our respective approaches to Israel, for example, although not at the heart of the relationship, presented an obvious case in point. The view that Israeli settlers building townships on occupied Palestinian land represented a new form of apartheid had gained a respectable currency in some South African political circles, including among officials of South Africa's foreign ministry, DIRCO. Arguable but not truly analogous, this perspective was not endorsed by Canadian governments, Liberal or Conservative, and the Harper government's particularly unquestioning support of Israel under Benjamin Netanyahu made the gap even bigger

Canada sought to view constructively South Africa's new alliance in the BRICS with Brazil, Russia, India and China. But the uncritical regard in which Zuma seemed to hold Russia and China was disturbing, and Canada's relations with the then-model democracy of Brazil were fraught with several commercial difficulties. The Harper government had re-directed some of its international assistance away for previous African recipients and our limited assistance to a relatively wealthy South Africa for "capacity building" was also being trimmed.

While attending official national day receptions with some of South Africa's immediate neighbours, one entered a looking glass world. Mozambique, Angola and Namibia celebrated their victorious "armed struggles" for independence highlighting the assistance given them by the Soviet Union and East Germany. The national day for the Czech Republic was doubly ironic as tribute was paid to the assistance of a regime that the Czechs themselves had overturned. From the perspective of the ANC, they had won the Cold War and their leaders nostalgically fostered a "liberationist" worldview suspended in amber. The South African government, after having offered diplomatic support to Muammar Khadafy in his armed response to the "Arab Spring," strongly condemned the bombardment of Khadafy's forces by NATO, including by Canadian aircraft. DIRCO Deputy Minister Ebrahim Ebrahim would have nothing of the notion that intervention in Libya was to protect protestors opposing Khadafy, in an extension of the "responsibility to protect" doctrine. He quoted Thucydides: "The strong do what they will; the weak suffer what they must."

Shortly after arriving in South Africa, I heard my new contacts in DIRCO and senior officials in other ministries asking: "What has happened to Canada? Where are you? You are not what you were." This was not accompanied by any reflection that South Africa might have had a role in what appeared to be a dimming friendship.

Our increasingly brittle rapport came directly into the open in an otherwise minor contretemps over the ANC's annual January executive meeting. Ambassadors were often invited to attend some public events held on the margins of this meeting. January 8, 2011 was to mark the 99th anniversary of the ANC, and the party was beginning to draw up plans for its centenary. A formal invitation to attend the event was received on Friday, January 7. We made no last-minute plans to go.

The week after, we began to hear through contacts at DIRCO, that Canada's absence had been specifically and negatively noted. Some references appeared in the media. We decided not to answer the criticisms. In truth, attendance at a governing party's executive meeting hardly seemed a high priority. Diplomats often seek permission to attend party conventions as observers, as it helps us better understand a country's politics, but attendance at executive functions risks wandering into a grey area of partisan endorsement. We chose not to say so. Instead, a discreet silence seemed better advised. Nonetheless, government officials began to escalate their expressions of concern about Canada, and it was a clear signal of the Zuma government's dissatisfaction.

There was more trouble ahead. I had the pleasure of attending a book festival in the town of Richmond where Canadian writer Fred Stenson was to read from *The Great Karoo*, his novel about Canadians who fought in the 1899 to 1902 Anglo-Boer War. I was surprised when, after his presentation, Ahmed Kathrada, one of the anti-apartheid movement's most renowned activists, stood in the front row to lambaste Canadian officials for blocking a visit he planned to Canada. This refusal, he said, was due to a Canadian law that labelled the ANC a terrorist organization. Kathrada was eloquent in his accusation that Canada, which had strongly opposed apartheid and imposed economic sanctions against the old regime, was mistreating and disdaining him and so many other freedom fighters who had brought the Rainbow Nation into being. I knew of the proscription against ANC members, but this was the first instance, where I had been present to see Canada publicly castigated in an open forum. Not realizing I was in the room, Kathrada was almost apologetic when I approached him to advise that I had heard his remarks and that I appreciated his frankness. I promised that I would bring his criticisms to the attention of headquarters in Ottawa.

In fact, ANC members were not wholly prohibited from entering Canada. Only those who were members of the ANC before the 1994 election were caught in the net. The ANC had long advocated the overthrow of apartheid by "armed struggle" and such advocacy was seen by Canadian authorities as disqualifying applicants for entry. However, recognizing such a ban applied to the vast number of senior South African officials, including Nelson Mandela himself who was an honorary citizen of Canada, the government devised a scheme of special ministerial permits, known as "national-interest" letters, to over-ride the regulations. This "work-around" did not free the applicant from having to fill out a form acknowledging he or she had once been declared a criminal under apartheid-era laws. And the delays in receiving authorization through special ministerial permits could be long, causing uncertainty for the traveller and leading even to cancellation of visits. It was the view of high commissioner Dion and later her successor Gaston Barban that action be taken to resolve this matter, which was a significant irritant in the Canada-South Africa relationship.

What happened subsequently is a testimony to the enduring power and frequent intractability of Canadian security authorities. The subject was raised by President Zuma with Canada's Governor General David Johnston during a state visit to South Africa in May 2013. Liberal MP and former justice minister Irwin Cotler extracted from Immigration Minister Jason Kenney a commitment in the House of Commons to resolve the issue. With apparent political will on its side, an interdepartmental committee of officials was convened to find a solution. After months of meetings, a Global Affairs memo on the outcome revealed: "Discussions had been underway with CIC (Citizenship and Immigration Canada) on legislative amendments to the IRPA (Immigration and Refugee Protection Act) to eliminate all restrictions on admissibility based on membership in the ANC. Recently we were informed that these critical amendments did not survive a legal review and will not be implemented." There was no further follow-up. An immigration official familiar with the matter would later ask me rhetorically: "Do you think the government would want to announce legal amendments resulting in the admission of terrorists?" He did not equate the ANC with terrorism. But he was giving expression to views – apparently very stubbornly held – within certain quarters of the security world. I was astonished by the evidence of such blinkered rigidity.

$\star\ \star\ \star$

One of the most remarkable features of South African society I discovered was the extraordinary vigour of the media. Newspapers were particularly prominent, including the *Mail and Guardian*, the *Johannesburg Star*, the *Sunday Times*, *Business Day*, and *City Press*. The state-owned South African Broadcast Corporation (SABC) was cautious, even tame, but privately-owned broadcasters did not hold back. The business programming that I listened to often on Classic FM pulled few punches. This freewheeling media environment did not please Jacob Zuma however, nor many of his close associates in the ANC. His dissatisfaction led to his call for the creation of a national press council to regulate media. He also backed the creation of an ANC-owned daily *The New Age*, with the financial backing of the Gupta family, Indian businessmen whose corruption of Zuma and other ANC officials was later confirmed in spectacular fashion during an inquiry following Zuma's eventual ouster. A controversial journalist who worked for *The Sunday Times*, Mzilikazi waAfrika, was arrested outside his newspaper's offices and detained for several days in an unknown location following a series of articles drawing attention to questionable contracting practices of an ANC provincial premier. It was more and more apparent that President Zuma and associates in the ANC were taking steps to infringe on South African press freedom.

High commissioner Dion and I discussed this trend, and she advised that defence of media freedom should become an important theme of the high commission's outreach. One of the responsibilities of the political section of an embassy is to underline values that "likeminded" countries, such as South Africa and Canada, share. Pressing for respect of human rights abroad is strongly supported by many Canadians. Some see it, rather idealistically, as the very heart of foreign policy. But promotion of human rights is more than altruism; it is part and parcel of strengthening Canada's international security. Strong democracies rarely go to war against each other. This understanding was very much stressed by Lloyd Axworthy during his tenure as foreign minister between 1996 and 2000. What he described as the "human security agenda" became central to Canadian foreign policy. That Canadian embassies try to promote democratic values and the rule of law within host countries is an application of what is often referred to as "soft power." Whereas traditionally such activity may have been interpreted as interference in a country's domestic affairs, it is more often seen today as a legitimate means to influence behaviour and advance pragmatic diplomatic objectives. But that point of view is not always accepted by host countries.

Our concerns about President Zuma's direction on press freedom were shared by both the United States and the United Kingdom. US Ambassador Don Gip organized an in-house conference of other embassies to review the government's statements and plans. UK High Commissioner Nicola Brewer agreed with High Commissioner Dion to organize a public seminar on press freedoms and, pertinently, the different forms that press councils take – from state-organized and -supervised to professionally constituted bodies (Where they exist in Canada, they are provincial bodies, organized voluntarily by participating newspapers to adjudicate citizen complaints).

We assembled a roster of international speakers, including from Britain and Canada, and held a two-day seminar at Witwatersrand University. The event provided context to the debate on South Africa's parliamentary bill on media restrictions, legislation that eventually was focused on security of government information. Free speech advocates managed to fight that bill to a standstill, and the high commission and our diplomatic allies were pleased with the outcome.

Yet I wondered for some time whether at the seminar we'd gone one bridge too far. At the concluding reception, we had invited as feature speaker Jonathan Shapiro, the renowned political cartoonist who published under the pen name of Zapiro. Zapiro's work on Zuma was fearless and unrestrained. In his cartoons, Zuma always appeared with a shower head attached to his skull – a reminder of the ANC leader's testimony during his rape trial that, although he had sex unprotected, to avoid AIDs he took a shower afterwards. One of Zapiro's most famous cartoons depicted Zuma unbuckling his trousers before a supine image of Lady Justice. I don't think giving Zapiro the premier platform that day would have improved our relations with the presidency, although for conference participants the cartoonist was a star attraction.

President Zuma was not subtle when he appointed Mohau Pheko to be South Africa's new high commissioner to Canada. Pheko was the daughter of a Pan African Congress (PAC) activist. The PAC had been a rival to the ANC during the anti-apartheid struggle. It had played a brave role in key confrontations but had frequently differed strategically from the ANC and unlike the Mandela-led organization, the PAC was not multi-racial; its membership always excluded whites. The appointment was seen nevertheless as acknowledging the PAC's significant and historic role and particularly of Pheko's father, Motsoko, who was a onetime PAC president.

Mohau Pheko's credentials were less than sterling. She claimed a PhD, which happened to come from a dubious US diploma mill, and she had recently been dropped as a columnist from the *Johannesburg Star* for plagiarism. The high commission discreetly honoured her appointment by offering a lunch at the official residence where she sought to show an earnest interest in education and social development. Shortly after she arrived in Ottawa however, Pheko began a concerted public campaign against the Harper government's stance on climate change. She certainly had a vulnerable target. The government had little intention of trying to comply with the Chrétien government's earlier unfulfilled commitment to meet specific targets for reducing greenhouse emissions under the multilateral Kyoto convention. And it was rumoured that Prime Minister Harper would announce Canada's withdrawal from the climate change agreement. Still, for the new South African high commissioner to publicly confront the government did not win friends and influence people in Ottawa. In a series of interviews given to Canadian media, Pheko accused Peter Kent, then the environment minister, of "bullying" countries to turn against Kyoto ahead of the annual Conference of the Parties (COP) to be held in the South African city of Durban in December 2011. She labelled Canada as "a brat" for threatening to pull out of the agreement.[5]

I made an appointment with John Davies, then the director in DIRCO of Canada-US relations. The high commission wanted to know whether the South African ambassador was "free-lancing" or whether she was expressing the official views of the government. Davies, a consummately courteous long-term veteran of the diplomatic service, did not give me a clear answer, promising to inquire further through his chain of command.

But I underlined that, as he well knew, it is generally assumed that ambassadors are speaking under the instructions of their governments.

That weekend Kent arrived in Johannesburg *en route* to the Durban conference. In the airport's VIP lounge, his staff passed on to me instructions from the Prime Minister's office for the high commission to go in again to DIRCO to formally protest Pheko's behaviour. With high commissioner Dion already in Durban, I was to be the messenger. I returned to see Davies to express Canada's considerable disappointment with the high commissioner's publicly critical statements. Having to scold the comportment of an ambassador is a rare event. But Pheko's public campaign was also highly unusual. Ambassadors usually find more discreet ways to deliver their government's messages. It gave me no pleasure to complain of her posturing, and it did not bode well for an improvement in a bilateral relationship that was already suffering badly.

Upon his return from Durban, Kent announced, as had been rumoured, Canada's withdrawal from the Kyoto Protocol. Those livid over the Harper government's climate change stance may have applauded Pheko's criticism. But from the perspective of effective diplomacy, where strong messages can be delivered directly to interlocutors behind closed doors while keeping powder dry to further future interests, Pheko tossed out the proverbial handbook. Recognizing that her usefulness in Ottawa was so quickly squandered, President Zuma, before too long, re-assigned her as ambassador to Japan.

Although no diplomatic "irritant" compared to the Pheko affair, there were others that still made our lives difficult. In 2011, the President of Côte D'Ivoire, Laurent Gbagbo, was vanquished in a United Nations-supervised democratic election. He refused to cede power. The Economic Union of West African States and the African Union endorsed the election results, which delivered Gbagbo's rival Allesame Outtara 54 per cent of the national vote. Gbagbo's refusal to step down accompanied by military manoeuvres that physically isolated Outtara and his closest followers presaged the outbreak of a new civil war. South Africa's response to Gbagbo's recalcitrance was not to condemn it, but to dispatch former president Thabo Mbeki to try to negotiate a government of national unity.

Canada found Gbagbo's ploy to retain power egregious and South Africa's initiative retrograde. Foreign Affairs' director general for Africa, Isabelle Roy, was dispatched to Pretoria, and I accompanied her to a meeting with DIRCO's Mdu Lembede, chief director for West Africa. "This goes beyond a local matter," Roy said. "It's a major democratic process important to the world generally . . . It is time for Gbagbo to leave peacefully." But Lembede was evasive; he cast doubt on the veracity of the UN-declared election results. "We do not have the facts to make a judgement on the issue. There are so many conflicting stories." It seemed South Africa saw a democratic transition of power as dispensable, that it could be put aside in the greater interest, in their view, of the cessation of violence. In this, they were following their model in neighbouring Zimbabwe when in 2009, Morgan Tsvangirai was forced into a power-sharing government with Robert Mugabe, even though election results indicated the latter had lost the election. Ironically, many ANC commentators on foreign policy were drawing revisionist lessons from their recent history. They pointed to the negotiations between the whites-only National Party government and the democratic coalition led by the ANC as the key to South Africa's transition to a non-racial democracy. Emphasizing the talks and not the principles, or the clear fact that the anti-apartheid struggle had been made more potent by the often harshly violent "people's war," was remarkably disingenuous. It had become a vogue for ANC members to refer to their policies as being inspired by the Zulu/Xhosa concept of "ubuntu" which refers to seeking social harmony in a shared humanity. I attended a seminar at the University of Pretoria where a South African academic compared ubuntu to Confucianism and its stress on the need to favour harmony over conflict. We are aware today of how the Communist Party of China, giving voice to similar allegedly Confucian precepts, subsumes the rights of individuals within a harmonious, yet authoritarian political structure. Roy appealed to Lembede "to support values and principles;" she meant upholding the results of a democratic election. The corollary was that applying them could mean Gbagbo's forcible removal from office, which South Africa would not endorse. In the end, Gbagbo was removed from office in April 2011 by forces supporting Ouattara, backed by French and UN armed forces. He was arraigned before the International Criminal

Court but acquitted in 2019. Ouattara went on to win re-election in 2015, chalking up 83.7 per cent of the vote.

⋆ ⋆ ⋆

Canada's trade relations with South Africa were managed by my energetic colleague, Barbara Giacomin, the senior trade commissioner, who was based 45 minutes from Pretoria in Johannesburg, South Africa's business hub. With her staff of Canadian and locally hired trade commissioners, it was her job to find opportunities for sales and investment by Canadian companies in South Africa. Mining suppliers and engineering firms were prominent among Giacomin's clients. Trade promotion was not central to my role, but I would become involved in commercial files when they were affected by government policies or regulations.

SNC Lavalin, the Canadian engineering firm which had taken over the previously Crown-owned Atomic Energy of Canada Ltd., as well as several other engineering firms, was interested in the prospective development of nuclear power in South Africa. South Africa already had significant nuclear assets. Two nuclear power stations were operated at Koeberg in the Western Cape, and a research reactor was located west of Pretoria at Pelindaba. South Africa's capabilities had permitted the apartheid regime to build six nuclear bombs in the '70s, later decommissioned during the transition to democracy, making South Africa the only country ever to have possessed and then destroyed its nuclear weaponry. I once had to visit the Pelindaba site to discuss with the facility's director Rob Adam international cooperation on the production of medical nuclear isotopes. In 2009, there was a world shortage, and Canada, with facilities in Chalk River, Ontario, and South Africa were cooperating to maintain a vital world supply. The potential for Canadian firms to participate in a South African nuclear power program was dependent, from Canada's perspective, on the signature of a nuclear cooperation agreement that would hold the signatories to peaceful uses and certain technical conditions, including a limitation on the percentage concentration of enriched uranium in any project. A draft agreement had been negotiated before I arrived in South Africa, but it became difficult for us to understand, as the months wore on, why we couldn't get South African officials to the table for the final signature. When we asked, our contacts at DIRCO explained that other departments in the government had responsibility for finalizing the text and having it vetted by authorities in the justice ministry. As time wore on, however, answers to our inquiries became increasingly circular, if not byzantine, and we realized we would have to engage senior decision-makers and activate some political will.

A visit to South Africa by our deputy minister of foreign affairs, Morris Rosenberg, provided just that opportunity. Barbara Thompson, an elected member of parliament and the deputy minister of energy, agreed to meet us in Cape Town. We arrived at a small hotel conference room where a sumptuous spread of hors d'oeuvres and sweets had been laid out on a large buffet table. We were rather astonished since the meeting was intended as a working session to get to the bottom of whatever reservations the South Africans were still harbouring.

About half an hour after the scheduled start of the meeting, the South African deputy minister arrived trailing a retinue of some dozen aides and junior officials. Everyone took a plate from the lavish buffet to at least acknowledge the courtesy being offered. Then Rosenberg moved to the business at hand. To our amazement, Minister Thompson seemed entirely unaware of any of the preceding efforts to identify the source of obstruction to the agreement. Then she turned to one of her aides to comment on the specific issue of the percentage threshold of enriched uranium. He had no specifics to provide either and unhelpfully undertook to consult officials in another ministry in the days to come. I probably surprised Rosenberg after the meeting when on the street and out of earshot of our hosts, I declared intemperately that the minister was either unacceptably ignorant or plainly lying.

The high commission had followed extensive diplomatic exchanges between the South African government and Iran, including mutual exchanges of high-level visits of large government delegations. There was also some evident Iranian interest in investing in uranium holdings that had once been held by Canadian investors. We were uneasy that some South Africans may have seen opportunities to participate in Iran's production of highly enriched uranium for a weapons program. (This preceded the eventual agreement of the United States and several European Union countries with Iran to curtail Iran's weapons program.)

But South Africa's reluctance to engage with us may have been more related to the deal that President Zuma was intent on developing with Russia to build a whole new fleet of nuclear reactors. Without a nuclear cooperation agreement, Canadian would-be investors would have been unable to bid on either reactor construction or even to supply technology or services. Several years later, Zuma's intentions in this area caused a rupture in his government when the South African treasurer Pravin Gordhan refused to endorse the necessary expenditures for Russian-built reactors. Zuma's single-minded attempts to drive his nuclear ambitions forward became one of the key factors that led to his resignation. The president's pointedly ignoring my face-to-face petition in Cape Town in 2011 was a silent evasion, for he was focused on bigger game.

There was one area during my four-year assignment in which cooperation between our governments never faltered. In the aftermath of the global financial crisis of 2008 and 2009, the G20 had agreed on measures to strengthen the world financial infrastructure. The banking systems of Canada and South Africa were among the few that suffered little damage during the crisis, partly due to strong prudential regulations. Neither country ventured far into the vast market of financial derivatives, many based on a dangerously mortgaged property sector, that lay at the base of the financial collapse. In advance of each G20 meeting, I was dispatched to the South African treasury to confirm whether Canada and South Africa shared perspectives regarding next moves to solidify the international finance. Among the key commitments made in the G20 was to strengthen national banking systems under the so-called Basel 3 rules to increase both bank capitalization and reserves. My meetings at Treasury were always a pleasure since both Canada and South Africa were at the forefront of efforts to comply. This was not a surprise, since during the nearly two decades of multi-racial democracy, South Africa's finance ministers had been diligent in maintaining balanced books, keeping government debt in tight check. Our common perspectives represented a calm oasis of mutual understanding in what otherwise had become a fractious relationship. Unfortunately, there were no guarantees that the South African treasury would remain an institution of economic orthodoxy within the South

African state and the degree of cooperation was in fact an aberration in a broadly strained relationship.

In retrospect, we were witnessing in South Africa a deep suspicion of the multilateral consensus that had so characterized the post-Cold War years. While going through the motions in its relations with Canada – as with the United States and the European Union as well – President Zuma's administration was more attracted to the policies of the state-dominated BRIC economies, Russia and China in particular. There was frustration in the ANC that, after years of supposedly market-oriented economic policies, South Africa had made little headway in reducing the widespread poverty of much of its black population. In that, the attitudes of many in the ANC were aligned with that of many citizen movements worldwide, disappointed that economic growth was not distributing its benefits in a more equitable fashion. How then to intelligently engage South Africa? Could a consensus embracing multilateralism be restored in face of the centrifugal forces of more authoritarian and protectionist attitudes worldwide? My faith in the future of South Africa and President Zuma's international choices was being stretched thin. Could Canada and South Africa become compatible partners again?

A Visit, a Funeral and an Elegy (2013–2014)

Governor General David Johnston was effusive. "I have made a very strong friendship with President Zuma that will last forever." He had just emerged from a formal *tête-à-tête* with Zuma, a key moment in his state visit to South Africa in May 2013. Diplomacy demands honeyed utterances. I had to admire this one, offered without even a hint of insincerity. A man of unfailing charm, Johnston is also down-to-earth and direct, conveys usually an optimistic outlook, and, as a former academic, he is eager to share his insights. Zuma and he bonded, it was said, through a discussion of their own children's school experiences. Improving Canada-South Africa cooperation in education was a key theme of his official visit.

Johnston also disclosed that he had recommended to Zuma a book entitled *Why Nations Fail* by economists Darus Acemoglu and James A. Robinson.[1] I quietly appreciated his finesse in conveying Canada's concern about South Africa's uncertain political trajectory while referencing a then-current bestseller. If Zuma had been discomfited by implied criticism, he seemed not to show it.

Shortly after the news conference in which Johnson proclaimed his friendship with Zuma, the two men hosted a formal luncheon attended by an array of South African and Canadian guests. It was a conclusion to a morning of pomp and circumstance. A ceremonial welcome had taken place at the Parliamentary precinct in Cape Town under magnificent sunshine. A military band was on hand to play *O Canada*, and the 21-gun salute echoed off the cliffs of nearby Table Mountain.

The visit had been a long time in the making. High Commissioner Dion declared from the beginning of her tenure in Pretoria that a high-level visit would be vital to put the Canada-South Africa relationship on a happier footing. Such orchestrated affairs are often considered the tried-and-true measure of the health of bilateral relations. Some think them antiquated diplomatic showpieces for the performance of a series of practised gestures. But governments do regard them as a common currency of foreign relations. And with goodwill on both sides, positive outcomes are possible.

The visit was the culmination of four years of sometimes frustrating effort. The protagonist needn't have been the governor general. The embassy would have been delighted with a visit by the prime minister but a senior departmental official visiting South Africa who had been brought into discussions with the prime minister early in his mandate recalled Harper asking why he should meet leaders with compromised or unsavoury reputations. He said the prime minister was not talking about South Africa. But the implication was that the reservations expressed would encompass President Zuma. In the face of such unease, it appeared pursuing a prime minister's visit might prove a lost cause.

Still, a foreign minister would have made a suitable impression. And in fact, that's where we started. John Baird, who was long a member of Prime Minister Harper's inner cabinet, was appointed to the role in 2011. Baird's pugnacity was well-known. He was perhaps the only Harper minister given license to engage in unscripted combat with the opposition in the House of Commons. He was deeply partisan. As a member of Parliament from an Ottawa constituency, he didn't limit himself to wielding only his regular ministerial responsibilities. His manoeuvring to assist a Conservative candidate for Ottawa's mayoralty unseat the Liberal incumbent was brutally transparent and effectively delayed the national capital's light rail system for a decade. His mark was made instantly at Foreign Affairs when he insisted that a wide swath of budgeted expenditures be reviewed directly by his office. His was a little-hidden strategy of cutting spending through delay, irrespective of the impact on programs. Foreign ministers normally undertake a series of foreign visits based on policy priorities. But his choice of destinations was capricious, often decided upon at the last minute and undertaken without senior departmental advisers.

Baird's mercurial nature notwithstanding, the high commission was eager to get his attention and persuade him of the value of an official visit to South Africa. Known for exercising considerable charm once engaged, Baird would likely make a good impression on his South African interlocutors.

Certainly, the foreign policy rationale was there. Approved language in briefing notes, speeches, and memoranda always declared South Africa an important political and trade partner. There was the potential for greater trade and investment. The country was a rare exemplar in Africa of democracy, the rule of law and individual freedom. We also needed to increase our dialogue on broader international issues. Could we be allies, rather than disillusioned friends, once again?

Our efforts to win Baird over did not run smooth. There was a rather awkward contretemps in the high commission's efforts to organize a seminar on Canada-South Africa relations. In partnership with David Hornsby, a Canadian international relations professor at Witwatersrand University (Wits) in Johannesburg, we would bring together Canadian and South African academics and government officials to review the evolution of relations over the years. We would begin with the apartheid era and proceed through the transition to democracy and up to the present. We looked to several sources of funds which included a conference budget that Hornsby was able to acquire from his program at Wits as well as high commission and headquarters funds that could be earmarked for these kinds of initiatives. One of the sources was going to be a sum from the "post initiative fund," or PIF, an allotment made available to the high commission but – under new rules – now requiring approval from Baird's office.

The submission was not well received. We were advised that the minister Baird did not care to see PIF funds go to "talking shops." He would not approve PIF funds for this purpose. Though disappointing, this was not fatal. I was able to obtain money from a Canadian studies program, overseen by headquarters, that was being wound down but still had some cash in the kitty. Also, Hornsby was able to identify some additional money from the university. With a somewhat reduced budget, we were still able to proceed.

On the eve of the meeting, our geographic desk in Ottawa sent us word that a senior aide in Baird's office was furious. It was the aide's understanding that the minister had forbidden the seminar from going ahead. This was not the high commission's view. We were proceeding with goodwill, abiding simply by the order not to use PIF funds.

However, information about the seminar had come to the minister's office by a circuitous route. Hornsby's father who was active in local politics in Guelph, Ontario, had expressed to local Conservative MP Michael Chong his pleasure that the high commission was working with his son in organizing the seminar. Chong, in turn, sent a note to Minister Baird congratulating him on his department's financial support. The minister's office swiftly reacted, asking my colleagues on the geographic desk why the seminar was proceeding when, in his view, the minister forbade it.

In the following weeks, I spent many hours explaining to the department's accountants – who were nervously reacting to the tremors from Baird's office – that the denial of PIF funding hadn't constituted a prohibition of the event. We considered the use of other available sources, including the funds provided by Wits University. If Baird didn't like using certain funds to pay for seminars, the high commission could still use its judgement that the event could further our objective of improving relations.

The seminar did not begin well. Several Canadian academics who had been critical in the '70s of Canada's continued relations with the apartheid regime seemed intent on revelling in a virtuous display of self-righteousness. They took numerous potshots at what they considered Canada's only tepid opposition to apartheid. As one South African colleague put it, the opening half-day was "a very long awkward moment." I began to wonder whether the minister's suspicion of talking shops had some merit. However, later sessions dealing with more current relations generated a much more constructive dialogue. There was a reconciliation of sorts between one of the older anti-apartheid activists and Glen Babb, the controversial former South African high commissioner to Canada, who had infamously conducted his own visits to Canadian Indian reserves in the late '80s to make a provocative comparison with apartheid. They had found common ground over the important role of education in addressing inequality. The participation of many of our colleagues from DIRCO helped to plant some seeds of greater trust between us.

In December 2012, I attended the ANC's five-year leadership convention in Mangaung, the municipality surrounding the better-known city of

Bloemfontein, which is South Africa's judicial capital. The main event was held under a giant marquee on the university grounds in the sweltering heat of the imminent South African summer. Floor demonstrations of North American political conventions have only a pale resemblance to the ANC's equivalents. Delegates sing in elaborate call and response choruses with lyrics that are traditional but also adapted to the political themes at play. Phalanxes of delegates dance in rhythm, surging forward and back in the hall.[2] "Yinde lendlela esiyiambayo" (The path is long) "Kwasho nMandela kulalendeli bahke" (Said Mandela to his followers) When President Zuma is on stage, he leads the delegates in this song and dance in an impressive display of improvisatory musical theatre. Zuma is rewarded by an extemporaneous song in his honour, "KuZuma sithembe" (In Zuma we trust). The chants are not always so exalted. Some delegates lament they haven't received their per diems. "Asinamali" (We have no money) "Sinaklo kaphela uqweqe lwesinkwa" (All we have are crusts).[3]

It was in such an atmosphere that I received a Blackberry message from headquarters advising me that Baird had selected a date to visit South Africa. I was instructed to contact the foreign minister, Maite Nkosana-Mashabane, to determine if she could receive him. I do not recall the exact date identified, but I knew that it had already been excluded as a possibility because of Mashabane's own schedule. Although already informed of this in previous communications, it seemed to be of no consequence to Baird's office. Moreover, it was said, Baird wanted a positive answer that very day.

I could see Mashabane on the convention floor, but it would be difficult to work my way through the singing and dancing throng. I waited for a break in the proceedings, then hurried to the exit that she was taking. I caught up with her on the crowded lawn outside the marquee. Knowing that I had no opportunity for more than a minimum of courtesies, I asked if she could meet Baird on the specified date. "It is so good to hear from my good friend John Baird," she smiled. Of course, they had crossed paths at international forums such as the United Nations General Assembly. She said the date in question might not be possible. But she advised me to contact her appointments secretary in Pretoria.

Mashabane knew me from previous meetings. I had drawn on part of my reserve of goodwill to buttonhole her in this setting. I think she recognized that I was acting on peremptory instructions. Ever the experienced diplomat, she would not tell me "no" directly. Of course, when I called her appointments secretary, she confirmed Mashabane's unavailability, which I dutifully relayed to headquarters.

It was gratifying to us when the prime minister's office finally approved a state visit by Governor-General David Johnston for early 2013. If the prime minister could not make the trip, we knew at least that a visit from Johnston would likely be carried off with professional style, though discussion of many policy issues would be circumscribed by his ceremonial role. We organized a high commission team to work with our department's and the governor-general's protocol offices to develop a program with our South African counterparts. The themes would emphasize technological innovation and education, in keeping with Johnston's particular interests and background as a university teacher and former president of both McGill and Waterloo universities. He would arrive in South Africa on May 19, after visits to Ghana and Botswana.

A key component of his program was to be an address to the South African Parliament on May 20, an event that we had meticulously choreographed in advance with the head of Parliament's protocol office. On Friday afternoon, May 17, I received a phone call from the director of the Canada desk at DIRCO, Royce Kuzwayo, who advised me that the speech to Parliament was being called off. Questions had been raised by senior members of the ANC, I was told. They wondered why Canada was to be given this distinct honour. Clearly despite our ongoing efforts, we still needed to contend with South African authorities' diffidence. Kuzwayo was blunt in saying that no other head of state on recent visits had spoken to Parliament, which included in 2012 and 2013, Ghana, Tanzania, Equatorial Guinea, Uganda, Nigeria, Namibia and, more significantly, India and China. Such comparisons had not been made in any of our planning with DIRCO and Parliament, and to be told of this major program change on the eve of the governor-general's arrival, left us in a major quandary. There was now a gaping hole in what had been a carefully planned program, a hole that had not been filled when the governor-general's flight touched down in Cape Town.

On news of the speech cancellation, the high commission's public affairs manager, Valery Yiptong, swung into action. She contacted the ever-helpful Professor Hornsby who agreed – on clearly very short notice – to host a speech by the governor general at Wits University. This would entail a rushed flight to Pretoria after a diplomatic lunch hosted by Zuma and a previously unplanned motorcade from Pretoria to Johannesburg. When the time came, I was relieved to be riding in the speeding police-escorted motorcade on the Pretoria-Joburg freeway, heading from the military airport to the Wits campus. We arrived at the international studies centre at Wits to be greeted by a packed hall.

Johnston's delegation included several representatives of Canadian educational institutions and non-governmental organizations with an interest in social development. His visit stimulated some interest in cooperation on a variety of fronts with respect to education and technology. Probably the most concrete outcomes of his visit were closer ties between the African Institute for Mathematical Sciences in Cape Town and the Perimeter Institute in Waterloo, Ontario. Additionally, Johnston encouraged Canadian and South African cooperation on the development of the Square Kilometre Array Telescope, which months later came to fruition in an important international agreement. Both these developments underlined the high levels of academic achievement for which in knowledgeable circles South Africa is still renowned.

Johnson was also able to increase the profile of Canadian business. He visited the Johannesburg stock exchange where he met Canadian businesses active in South Africa. Although Canadian investment in South Africa had been faltering, there was still a strong two-way-trade in equipment and services, largely related to the mining sector. And the governor-general also rode the recently opened Johannesburg-to-Pretoria high-speed train, or Gautrain, built by Canada's trains-and-planes manufacturer, Bombardier. Johnston's visit did not in itself repair the wear and tear on the Canada-South Africa relationship. But it was a starting point to re-charge a friendship that both countries perceived as faltering.

I never had the honour of meeting Nelson Mandela. During my assignment in South Africa, he was living in almost complete seclusion with his wife Graça Machel in a house in the upscale Johannesburg neighbourhood of Houghton. The renowned leader of the anti-apartheid struggle and the first president of South Africa's multi-racial democracy was afflicted by dementia that neither his family nor his ANC comrades would acknowledge.[4] The struggle "icon," as he was frequently labelled, was continuing to dispense words of wisdom to the country's rulers, according to the myth-making narrative coming from various authorities. [5] His rare appearances suggested otherwise. Graça Machel physically waved his hand for him as he was driven by golf cart into the closing ceremonies of the 2010 World Cup watched by millions of South Africans on television. President Zuma and several of his cabinet ministers shamelessly posed for photos around his vacantly smiling figure while claiming to have visited him to get his political advice. No one would publicly acknowledge his diminished cognitive capacities. It was his indispensable leadership that had led South Africa through a largely non-violent transition from racist tyranny to political equality and democratic freedom. Many feared for the future of South Africa without his guiding hand.

From the outset, my highest priority as political counsellor, as high commissioner Dion stressed to me, was to plan for Canada's participation in Nelson Mandela's funeral. The challenge was dealing with the complete reticence of South African authorities. They would offer not the slightest hint they were making any preparations for Mandela's death. No one would utter a word about the ailing health of Madiba, using the honorific tribal name spoken always with great reverence. Every one of the approximately 120 foreign embassies in Pretoria knew Mandela's funeral would be an enormous, logistically challenging event. Mandela's international prominence and the saintly regard in which he was held everywhere meant few countries would not want their leaders present. Our view at the high commission, and shared by headquarters, was that Prime Minister Harper must attend. We knew Governor-General Johnston would also be a choice. But given the greater political weight of the prime minister, as perceived not just in Canada but abroad, we believed, for the sake of our relations with South Africa, that Prime Minister Harper should be our principal designated mourner.

We were uncertain as to his receptivity to performing this role. His degree of appreciation of South Africa and its history was unknown. During

South Africa's democratic transition, Stephen Harper was organizing the newly formed Reform Party. He served as a Reform MP between 1993 and 1997. The Reform Party's focus on strengthening Canada's regions and promoting fiscal conservatism included little attention to foreign policy. When Nelson Mandela was awarded honorary Canadian citizenship in 1998, Harper, no longer in the House of Commons, was head of the National Citizen's Coalition, a conservative think tank with strong economic priorities. I was not convinced the prime minister, whose political focus had always been domestic, would be easily persuaded to attend the funeral. But working closely with the foreign affairs advisers in the privy council office, we obtained an early affirmative response. It came with the important and understandable proviso that the prime minister be informed immediately upon Mandela's death so that he could issue a statement of consolation without delay. That statement would also initiate the logistics for his funeral attendance.

Mandela was rushed to hospital on several occasions starting in 2011. The government and family being ever protective of his privacy, the nature of these crises was not revealed, other than usually vague references to respiratory issues (he had survived tuberculosis contracted during his prison years on Robben Island). Each of these hospitalizations triggered panic among the embassies in Pretoria. At no point had the government revealed any of its contingency plans for a funeral, and few missions were able to get guarantees to book the many hotel rooms and vehicles that senior delegations would need on short notice.

After a sudden hospitalization in March 2013, the embargo on public statements began to fracture. Conflicting fragments of information about Mandela's health started to appear. It became evident that the many parties who had a direct interest in Mandela's health were not unanimous on how to communicate with the public. There were views of the immediate family, his current wife Graça Machel and the various Mandela children from his two previous marriages; of the ANC, both party and government leaders; and of the Nelson Mandela Foundation, established by Mandela to protect and further his legacy. After an agreement that South African vice president Kgalema Motlanthe should become the official spokesperson, the government at last decided to start talking about possible funeral arrangements, although not entirely transparently.

My colleague, Patrick Cram, the high commission's second secretary, and Colonel Richard Milot, the defence advisor, had to dig to find reliable sources in their respective networks. At last, some of the rudiments of the funeral planning began to take shape, including the locations, Pretoria City Hall and the Union Buildings, the office of the South African presidency, for his lying-in-state; Johannesburg's World Cup stadium for the public memorial service; and finally, Mandela's home village of Qunu for the formal ceremony and burial.

In June 2013, after another sudden admission to hospital, a rumour spread that Mandela was already dead and that the family, the government and the foundation were arguing over the funeral arrangements. Delaying the death announcement seemed far-fetched, but a recent incident involving neighbouring Malawi fed the rumour mill.[6] Less sensational than the rumour he was already dead was the claim that Mandela was being kept alive through medical intervention. This notion was fed by the statement by Mandela's oldest daughter from his first wife Evelyn that her father was "at peace." By being kept alive by extraordinary measures, the various "stakeholders" would have time to coordinate their efforts, the theory went.

The rumours and uncertainty sparked a reaction. Hotels we had had preliminary discussions with now became willing to enter into agreements to block rooms. Their readiness to enter into contracts allowed our headquarters to release funds so that an expected Canadian government delegation of some 80 people could attend. This would include Prime Minister Harper and former prime ministers Jean Chrétien, Brian Mulroney and Joe Clark, former governors-general Adrienne Clarkson and Michaëlle Jean, as well as the core staff of the prime minister's office to provide administrative support and security. The high commission assembled its own logistics team to manage local transport and accommodation as well as organize whatever parallel program would be needed for senior delegation members. Colonel Milot undertook an advance visit to Qunu in the Eastern Cape province.

As much as our deep respect for Mandela motivated our preparations for the funeral, we were also driven by our desire to resuscitate our relationship with South Africa. It was not evident that our fractious relationship could be readily repaired. But we could try to create an atmosphere in which we could do so. Participating fully in mourning the loss of this pivotal figure of freedom – the political liberator of his people, Nobel Peace Prize winner and honorary Canadian citizen – would be an important show of respect to South Africans and their country.

* * *

However, I did not have the opportunity to travel any further down reconciliation road. Suzanne and I left South Africa at the end of August of that year. Days following our departure, defying the pessimistic forecasts of so many, Mandela rallied and was released from his prolonged hospital stay. But his recovery would not last long; he had only a few more months to live. He died at home on December 5, 2013. The plans the high commission put in place for attendance at his funeral were implemented by high commissioner Barban and my successor, Brad Belanger.

In the weeks before our departure, the Johannesburg Symphony Choir presented Benjamin Britten's *Cantata on Saint Nicholas*. The tale of the death of the fourth-century churchman renowned for his care of the poor and oppressed seemed to resonate with the audience as it evoked what all knew would be the imminent passing of Madiba. "Let the legends that we tell praise him, and our prayers as well. We keep his memory alive in legends that our children, and their children's children, treasure still."

In the years following our departure from South Africa, the always rumoured deep corruption of the Zuma administration was spectacularly exposed. The Gupta family's complicated involvement with the Zuma family and their role in lining their pockets through "state capture" was the subject of the Zondo inquiry, called after Zuma was forced from office. One of the precipitating factors in his fall was his role in trying to hand Russia a major contract to build South African nuclear reactors.[7] Once the Zondo inquiry got rolling the magnitude of the misappropriation of funds under Zuma became almost awe-inspiring.[8]

Badly sideswiped in the revelations was the Canadian company Bombardier, which had persuaded Export Development Canada to lend the Guptas some $10.4 million to buy one of their corporate jets. A shadow was cast over Bombardier's much larger contract to sell locomotives to the South African government rail corporation Transnet. The high commission had been advised of Bombardier's interest in the Transnet bid about

2012. I had joined high commissioner Dion in a meeting with several of the company's representatives in the high commission's board room, where they outlined their objective of bidding on the Transnet tender. We encouraged them in their efforts. Evidence presented before the Zondo commission revealed that interventions by senior South African government officials were critical in denying Chinese firms an inside, exclusive track to the Transnet contract (it was eventually apportioned between two state-owned Chinese firms and Bombardier). Still, the tender was tainted by efforts at the highest level in Transnet to inflate the size of the contract and channel payments through Gupta family-controlled companies.[9]

The Zondo inquiry was an invaluable exercise in exposing the mechanics of Zuma's corrupt regime. In the late months of my assignment, a large Canadian resource company intent on exploration of promising structures in the South African offshore visited the high commission asking us to join it in a visit with Zuma to discuss the company plans. Word came later that Zuma preferred to meet the company alone without a Canadian high commission representative being present. Evidently what Zuma might propose was best kept from the Canadian government's prying eyes.

Governor General Johnston's veiled warning to Zuma in his reference to *Why Nations Fail* was not off the mark. Acemoglu's and Robinson's thesis is that nations that succeed establish a virtuous circle in which "inclusive" political institutions and "inclusive" economic institutions reinforce each other in processes of continually positive feedback. Zuma's government was on the verge of initiating a vicious circle, where his government was becoming an "extractive" political institution incentivising "extractive" economic behaviour by him and his cronies. But South Africa's political institutions still proved strong enough to derail Zuma's predations, so that the country's virtuous circle could be saved from becoming a vicious one.

From the point of view of South Africa's potential and its capacity to lead an African economic take-off, the Zuma years were lost years. Much hope was attached to his replacement, Cyril Ramaphosa, who, in addition to his being a prominent leader in the anti-apartheid movement, was a successful businessperson in the Rainbow Nation's early years. But the desire of many in the multi-faceted ANC alliance to reap the financial spoils of their political success and the strong attraction of the ANC to the

BRICS and China in particular, for its brand of state-sponsored growth, will weigh on Ramaphosa. Will South Africa again become a stronger partner with Canada in the rules-based international order characterized by free trade and open markets? Or will the siren song of managed trade and the dubious benefits of closer ties with authoritarian regimes (and the prospects of becoming a client state) prove more alluring?

A Canadian Gulliver Confronts an Arcane World (2009–2013)

Our motorcade of diplomatic vehicles, slightly ahead of schedule, drove slowly towards the Iavoloha presidential palace. My Japanese, South Korean, and European Union counterparts, as well as a representative of the African Development Bank and I, each travelled in our respective cars. My chauffeur was Monsieur David driving his immaculately maintained vintage blue Peugeot. I always called on his services on frequent visits to Madagascar and its capital Antananarivo.

On this occasion we were on our way to a meeting with Madagascar's president Andry Rajoelina. The palace is 15 kilometres to the south of Antananarivo located in hilly, forested terrain typical of the Madagascar highlands. We turned into the palace gates onto a long drive bordered by high baobab trees which, despite the attempt at splendour, looked desolate, their foliage at this time of year being only brown and scruffy tops of dead leaves. The immense white palace, a modern structure of North Korean design, dominated the end of the drive. The motorcade pulled into the palace courtyard. A grand outdoor staircase led to equally impressive doors and, entering, we saw on either side of the main entry hall, three-storey high vertical banners bearing the image of President Rajoelina.

Many Malagasies are descended from ocean-going Indonesian adventurers who settled the island centuries ago. French is the language of business here, but the Malagasy tongue has its roots in Sumatra and Java on the eastern edges of the Indian Ocean. The people have also been influenced by their centuries of contact with Arab and South Asian merchants who plied their trade with the island long before the arrival of Europeans in the 16th century. Madagascar is an African country with a difference.

The boyish, then 38-year-old president had been in tenuous charge of his country since early 2009. He was installed in office by a military coup that overthrew the elected president Marc Ravalomanana. Rajoelina, a successful media entrepreneur as well as past mayor of the capital, had rallied opposition to the Ravalomanana government, whose controversial free-market, but far from even-handed, economic measures, had not been good for some of Rajoelina's growing businesses. His rise to power on a wave of well-orchestrated protests eventually backed by a strong military faction drew rapid international condemnation. Madagascar was suspended from the African Union, the Southern African Development Community (SADC), and La Francophonie. International assistance, including from the World Bank, was put largely on hold. From its outset, Rajoelina's government was in quarantine. Many international partners, including the United States, Japan, South Korea, the European Union – and Canada – suspended full diplomatic relations with a view to pressuring Rajoelina to restore democracy.

The giant portraits in the palace, clearly meant to impress visitors with this man's domination of Madagascar's affairs, were at odds with his actual vulnerability. He was being pressed by the leaders of most of Madagascar's international partners not only to yield power, but also to agree not to present himself as a candidate to lead a subsequent democratic administration – the restoration of which was a condition, among others, of return to full membership in the African Union.

When I joined External in 1990, I would not have considered it likely, some 25 years later, that I'd be making a diplomatic representation to the putative head of state of the remote island nation of Madagascar. The country of 25 million people with one of the world's lowest per capita incomes (US$403 in 2015)[1] did not then figure prominently as a Canadian foreign policy priority. And up until my frequent visits after 2009, my own view of the country was limited to seeing it as an isolated, ecologically unique domain, home of some evolutionarily distinct primates known as lemurs, and endangered rain forests. I was to learn how much more intriguing than I imagined, Madagascar really was.

My visits there were very much in pursuit of Canadian interests, the most important of those being the more than $7-billion investment managed by the Canadian company Sherritt International. The company's

Ambatovy nickel and cobalt mine, and refinery were the product, at the time, of the largest single foreign investment in Madagascar.

Canada's suspension of full diplomatic relations with Madagascar after the coup meant that the Canadian high commissioner in South Africa, who is normally accredited to Madagascar as a non-resident ambassador, would not present credentials to the Malagasy authorities or hold official meetings with them. However, under such circumstances, for practical purposes, a Canadian representative must be available in the region to carry out essential business, and for that purpose, a "*chargé d'affaires*" is appointed. Shortly after my arrival in Pretoria, the Malagasy authorities were advised that I would perform that role.

Chargés are entrusted with necessary business regarding their countries' interests. Above all, that means helping any of their citizens in distress. The "consular cases" which had come to the Canadian high commission's attention in recent months threw some light on sinister facets of the Malagasy regime. A local businessman with dual Malagasy-Canadian citizenship had recently been released from jail. The authorities had accused him of being involved in a string of bombings around the capital in the aftermath of the 2009 coup. Little credible evidence had been made public, and there were suspicions that the explosions were orchestrated by the military to justify arrests of regime opponents. The businessman was married to a woman who had been a senior advisor to overthrown president Ravalomanana, and she had gone into hiding. Rather than the Malagasy-Canadian's arrest being tied to a genuine accusation, it was, we suspected, a means to bring his spouse into the open.

Another Canadian working as the health and safety officer of a Canadian company in Madagascar faced a different sort of jeopardy. In keeping with his role, he had been first on the scene of a fatality on the company job site. A local worker had been found dead in a secluded corner of an industrial plant near a series of pipes and conduits. Much to his surprise after reporting the accident, the health and safety manager was taken into custody and charged with murder. It turned out that members of the victim's family had pressed a local judge to proceed with an investigation. The Canadian health and safety officer was put in a position of singular jeopardy for what appeared to be dubious motives.

Such cases brought to the Canadian high commission's attention demonstrated that Malagasy authorities did not necessarily either abide by clear rules, or in many instances, have much regard for civil rights.[2] These were two of the cases I had to manage, with the very capable assistance of local high commission employees with extensive experience in consular matters.

But Canada's interests are not only restricted to assisting individual Canadians. Commercial interests are also at stake. In July 2011, my wife and I were in Ottawa for vacation, staying at my sister-in-law's home and taking the time to re-connect with family and friends. I received an e-mail from High Commissioner Dion asking me to contact Andrew McAlister, a former Global Affairs colleague now working as an independent consultant, whose client base included Sherritt. I called him at his home in Ottawa and he told me about negative signals from the Rajoelina government suggesting that it was not prepared to provide Ambatovy with its expected operating licence which it needed to start operations. The mine and refinery were near completion, and the licence was needed to begin tests to ensure the two complexes and the connecting slurry pipeline would work according to specifications. The government had raised safety issues with regard to possible gas leaks at the refinery and several other questions. As these matters had previously been addressed in official government inspections, there was the suspicion among Ambatovy managers that the Rajoelina government was manoeuvring to obtain a concession from the company, possibly in the form of some payment to the authorities. McAlister asked if the Canadian high commission would be willing to join our counterparts from Japan and South Korea, whose own companies, Sumitomo and Korean Resources (Kores), had significant stakes in Ambatovy, to make a direct representation, or *démarche*, to the Malagasy authorities – and, if possible, to Rajoelina himself. As company president Mark Plamondon was himself returning from summer vacation in Alberta to be on site to deal with the situation, I agreed to shorten my vacation to undertake this appeal.

It's a good day's journey from Pretoria to Antananarivo. The South African Airways flight leaves at 10 am and after a nearly four-hour crossing of the wide Mozambican Channel, the landscape of Madagascar opens below. On my first visit, I was struck by the massive rivers that flow westward from the highlands and, as I approached Tana, the cultivated fields which surround circular farm enclaves defined by wooden palisades. The road from Antananarivo's airport offers a fascinating introduction to the capital region. Small shops and homes, many with steep tiled roofs with upswept Asiatic eaves, abut the narrow, two-lane paved artery. Then the vista opens as the road follows the top of a dike running through extensive rice paddies spread over a plateau whose limits are defined in the distance by a series of flat-topped hills. Sharing the road are large, wooden two-wheeled carts, some pulled by zebus, curved-horn oxen; others by barefoot men. As we started to climb a hill towards the summit of the city, I saw four men, two between cart poles, two pushing from behind, hauling a full load of bricks. At times the road becomes so narrow, there is barely room for two vehicles to pass. It then traverses a crowded open-air market before reaching Lake Anosy, the artificial reservoir around which many of Madagascar's government buildings are located. The route continues up a narrow winding road to the hotel usually favoured by our staff from the high commission, La Varangue, only a stone's throw from the in-town presidential palace, Ambohisorohitra. After landing at 3 pm and the more than hour-long drive from the airport, late afternoon shadows lengthen, especially in July, the height of the southern hemisphere winter, a dry season with cooler temperatures. As night falls, the streets grow dark with little public lighting. La Varangue's award-winning restaurant offers a welcome retreat from the surrounding darkness.

I had arranged to visit the Japanese embassy the following day, where I was to meet the Japanese ambassador, my South Korean counterpart from Pretoria, and representatives of Ambatovy, including staff from Sumitomo and Kores. The embassy is a modern building reflecting the elegant simplicity common to Japanese official architecture. I was greeted by the second secretary and ushered into the ambassador's office. Ambassador Tetsuro Kawaguchi was an experienced diplomat. I had met him once previously and was struck by his excellent command of French and his facility as a raconteur. He was joined by his second-in-command, Shigeru Takuyasu, who, due to Japan's cessation of full diplomatic relations with Madagascar while still having a resident ambassador, had become the chief interlocutor with the Malagasies on any business requiring high-level contact.

Takuyasu would become a close ally over the next 18 months as the Malagasy political situation unfolded.

The purpose of the meeting was first to confirm that a *démarche* to the Malagasy government should be undertaken and then to agree on the nature of the message. Ambatovy president Plamondon and his government relations executive Juanita Montalvo were pleased with Japan's, South Korea's and Canada's unanimous agreement to undertake the formal intervention.

Speaking to foreign government authorities on behalf of Canadian companies is not a routine matter. The Canadian Trade Commissioner Service (TCS), the network of Canadian trade commissioners in our embassies abroad, categorizes such interventions as "enhanced services" which go beyond the market intelligence, contact referrals and trouble-shooting that constitute trade commissioners' "core services." Nonetheless, with clients whose businesses have significant impact on, and will bring benefit to, the Canadian economy, embassies will try to reach foreign government decisionmakers at the highest level to help resolve outstanding issues. Ambatovy's operation in Madagascar certainly qualified for enhanced service. At the same time, I recommended to my colleagues that the focus of our intervention should not strictly be on the interests of Sherritt, Sumitomo, and Kores, but rather on the impact the Rajoelina government's actions was having on Madagascar's international reputation and on its investment climate.

During the continuing delay in the authorization of the operating permit, Rajoelina's people had begun to show more of their hand. According to Montalvo, senior government officials had made blatantly clear that the cost of obtaining the permit would be $75 million. Ambatovy, on the other hand, was adamant that since the fiscal terms for building and operating the mine had been negotiated before the commencement of construction in conformity with the country's own Loi sur les Grands Investissements Miniers (LGIM), the company had no intention of producing such a gratuitous payment. Although a Chinese firm had recently been granted an iron ore concession in northern Madagascar by tendering a $100 million payment to the Malagasy treasury, on terms unrelated to the LGIM, Ambatovy was not going to be drawn into that game. What was now required was obtaining an audience with the palace to present our case. With his more extensive contacts, it fell on Takuyasu to seek the meeting.

Ambatovy was a corporate Gulliver held down by Lilliputian bonds. It was investing more than $6.6 billion in a major project that it couldn't simply abandon when faced with an unjustifiable demand. At the same time, Rajoelina was not exactly impregnable. His country was suffering as a result of the international withdrawal of aid. Madagascar had been cut out of all its regional alliances and La Francophonie. Its economy was shrinking, and it needed foreign investment. Rajoelina's authority was not based on any constitutional legitimacy, and it was not clear whether the business and military interests to which he seemed beholden would necessarily keep him in power. Paradoxically, a meeting with a diplomatic contingent from Japan, South Korea and Canada offered him some prestige and thereby some protection.

Confirmation of the meeting took several days while Tukuyasu worked his contacts in the foreign ministry and president's office. When it did come, it was late on a Thursday evening, for a meeting the following morning at the president's in-town palace. The building was at most a five-minute walk from my hotel, but to make an impression, we organized a diplomatic motorcade that descended through one-way streets to Lake Anosy and then re-mounted the hill by another road, crossed the palace square, and was then admitted through the palace's security gate. We were escorted to a large formal chamber to the right of the palace's main lobby. Company representatives had been summoned by the president's office for a later meeting and were already seated in an ante-room.

The youthful president of the Haute Autorité de la Transition (HAT, High Authority of the Transition), as his government was called, was seated with Finance Minister Héry Rajaonarimampianina and the presidential office's chief of protocol. Our three-country delegation sat in chairs at right angles to the president. We had agreed that Takuyusu and I would be the delegation spokespersons. I said:

> Thank you, your excellency for having received us today. The fact that you have given us this meeting is, we hope, an indication of the importance of this matter for you and your government. We regret that we must express our uneasiness with respect to

the absence of authorization for the company Ambatovy to start production. In North America we have the expression; 'You don't move the goalposts after the beginning of the game.' From our perspective that is exactly what is happening here.

As of today, it has been six weeks since Ambatovy fulfilled all the technical, economic and environmental requirements of the laws and regulations that Madagascar demands. And your minister responsible has certified that. Suddenly there comes a new demand for another review that didn't previously exist in the approval process. Ambatovy believed that it possessed the certificates required under the Law of Large Mining Investments. Suddenly, after an investment of $6.6 billion, the requisite certificate was withheld.

Mister President, we believe that you have the interests and aspirations of the Malagasy people at heart. The Ambatovy project is delivering and will deliver to the people of Madagascar jobs, business contracts and government revenues that will increase Madagascar's prosperity.

If you will further permit me, excellency, the decision to withdraw Ambatovy's authorization to proceed with its project will have a major impact on your country's investment climate. Already some companies appear uneasy about risking their money here.[3]

Rajoelina listened politely through this admittedly stern presentation, a little less nuanced than I would have been able to make in English, but still reflecting the gravity with which we viewed the matter. My Japanese colleague intervened somewhat more smoothly to make a similar case for the need of a stable regulatory climate to attract investment. The meeting lasted less than half an hour; Rajoelina thanked us and agreed to take our views under consideration. We departed, after a few pleasantries.

We had agreed to meet Plamondon and his Ambatovy team in a small board room in the La Varangue Hotel following their own audience with Rajoelina. When they appeared after another half-hour, they looked relieved, but not elated. Rajoelina had agreed to provide the company with its required permit to start operations. There were conditions. It was a six-month, temporary permit, although renewable indefinitely. Rajoelina had saved face but, unfortunately for the company, left the door open to further harassment down the road. For now, though, our efforts could be taken as a victory. Acknowledging that this was only a temporary win, I was still sufficiently satisfied and immediately transmitted the results by Blackberry to High Commissioner Dion in Pretoria. Later that day I watched the waters of the Mozambican Channel on my flight back to Pretoria. I deemed our intervention had been work well done. But it was only one step in a struggle with Rajoelina that was bound to continue.

On November 17, 2010, senior officers at an army base near Tana's international airport said they had seized control of the facility and were calling on other regiments to rise in opposition to the government. Within less than 24 hours, troops loyal to Rajoelina had re-taken the base, and the poorly planned uprising was suppressed. Nonetheless the would-be coup served to underline the continuing illegitimacy of the government, and increased pressure on both the regime and various international mediators who were trying to find a way out of the ongoing "crise," to which the situation was now universally referred. By late 2011, the Southern African Development Community (SADC) had negotiated a significant step forward in getting Rajoelina to sign on to most elements of a "road map" toward restoration of democracy. Among other measures, Rajoelina had appointed to a newly designed Congress, deputies and senators representing a broad cross-section of many of the larger political parties, or *mouvances*, and had further appointed a prime minister who had their broad support, in what was now called, not the HAT, but the Government of Consensus. What remained outstanding were agreements to call elections; ensure that they were free and fair; provide amnesty for political opponents; and, most difficult of all, accept that neither Rajoelina nor his arch-rival Ravalolamana would present themselves as candidates for the presidency.

Into this mix now stepped La Francophonie, which during its summit in Switzerland from October 22 to 24, 2010, committed to send a mission to Madagascar to see if it could contribute to the resolution of "la crise." Canada's ambassador to La Francophonie was Philippe Beaulne, who was also our ambassador to Romania. I was to meet him in Tana to provide a briefing on the situation and participate in several of the delegation meetings. The Francophonie mission took place from March 4 to 9, 2012 and included meetings with the South African embassy, which was guiding the SADC mediation process; other relevant missions including France and the European Union; the Malagasy foreign ministry; and most importantly the prime minister of the consensus, Omer Beriziky, and President Rajoelina.

La Francophonie's role and purpose may sometimes seem abstract or even obscure to many Canadians. But its mission was intended to play a role in moving Madagascar back towards democratic norms. Still, it was surprising to me how La Francophonie's role was being deeply misconstrued in some quarters. During the mission, I had my own meetings with both the chargés of the United States and the United Kingdom. Both made the surprising assertion that the Francophonie mission was part of a scheme by France to undermine the SADC road map and open the way to acceptance by the international community of inadequately organized and effectively sham elections. Underlying this perspective was the suspicion that Rajoelina's coup had been backed by the French, and that French business interests were benefiting through a close relationship with the president and his circle. It was true the French embassy throughout most of the crisis had pulled its punches in refraining from criticizing the regime too harshly. French relations with Ravalomanana had been fractious, and Ravalomanana had expelled the French ambassador of the time, leaving a real sense of rancour in the relationship. However, with the defeat of President Sarkozy and the ascendance of President François Hollande, the French embassy in Madagascar had become increasingly aligned with its EU partners, South Africa and SADC, the United States, and Canada.

I stressed to both the US and UK chargés that they misunderstood both the role of the Francophonie and its present mission. Canada, I noted, was an important and influential member of the Francophonie and neither we nor other members were in Madagascar to support a phony solution to "la crise." The presence of the delegation was fulfillment of the promise made by Francophonie ministers at the last summit to send a mission to assess how well the road map was being implemented. In fact, that promise blocked a premature proposal by France to "re-integrate" Madagascar as a Francophonie member based on partial progress toward democratic restoration. The full participation of France on the current mission meant that it had accepted both Ravalomanana's right to return and an amnesty for his supporters.

Perhaps my US and UK counterparts were not convinced. But for me it was a lesson in how honest efforts can at times be deeply misunderstood. It also made clear the importance of effective communication and dialogue.

The Francophonie visit proved a success. The delegation assessed that there was sufficient goodwill among the relevant Malagasy parties to move toward resolution of "la crise" through new elections. And they offered La Francophonie's assistance in organizing them.

These positive developments were leading to decisions by many countries to resume their official relations with the Malagasy government. The UK, Australia, Mauritius, and Japan announced that they were prepared to present their diplomatic credentials under new ambassadors. The South Koreans, who like Canada were managing their relations from their embassy in Pretoria, were eager to learn what Canada's stance would be. Although the high commission was recommending to headquarters a review of Canada's position and the possibility that the high commissioner would present credentials in Tana, we had not yet received positive instructions in that regard. In the meantime, more pressing for us, was the appointment of an honorary consul in Madagascar who would be able to attend more expeditiously to consular matters than our remote high commission team based in Pretoria could.

Of course, the decision for Canada relative to re-establishment of relations was not only predicated upon Madagascar's compliance with the "road map" but also to the security of Canadian investments, including Ambatovy. Senior management at Ambatovy believed that its interests would better be protected by a fulltime diplomatic presence in Tana. There was however the alternate view that withholding full diplomatic recognition would continue to exert pressure on a government that was eager to be legitimized. And the only course for re-establishing legitimacy was through elections. An elected, constitutional government might also be more constrained by law in its actions towards investors.

But these considerations became secondary when the next shoe dropped in Rajoelina's campaign to extract concessions from Ambatovy.

Nearly a year after his government had granted the company a temporary permit, it once again pushed the firm back into uncertain territory. The "indefinitely" renewable permit had not been renewed, and the government was now choosing to re-interpret its own laws to extract additional revenues. It was time once again to return to Tana to regroup with our partners to respond to this latest development.[4]

When Rajoelina's government began to re-interpret its own laws, there were serious repercussions that went beyond mining projects' internal viability. Under the LGIM, the government imposed a two per cent royalty on revenues generated from the sales of ore. Of this royalty 0.6 per cent was dispensed directly to the commune, or municipality, in which the ore is mined. The remaining 1.4 per cent went to the central treasury. However, if the ore is refined in Madagascar, the royalty was cut in half, and only one per cent was imposed as a tax on the product. However, according to the government's new interpretation, the 50 per cent royalty reduction only applied to the portion of the royalty paid to the commune. Thus, the municipality would receive the anticipated 0.3 per cent royalty from sales. But the central treasury's share would be unreduced, meaning the mine would be paying a royalty 60 per cent higher than planned.

In addition to this unexpected burden, the treasury was withholding reimbursements of value-added tax paid by mining exporters to their Malagasy suppliers. Value-added tax is intended to be fully borne by final purchasers, and as it cascades through the system from original producers to ultimate buyers, the portion paid by intermediaries is refunded to them. However, where a good is sold for export, the sales tax is not collected from the buyer, and the exporter is entitled to a reimbursement in the same manner as all its suppliers. This sum was being withheld by the treasury.

Ambatovy was a project almost entirely financed by debt. Its financiers included nine commercial banks plus the government-backed African Development Bank, Export Development Canada, Export-Import Bank of Korea, Japan Bank of International Cooperation, and the European Investment Bank. Since the changes imposed by the Malagasy government would hurt the project's revenues, they also affected its ability to pay its debts. And since the loans had been made based on assumptions related to the original tax framework, the creditors had become concerned.

We convened in the offices of the European Union to consider a new *démarche*. We needed to make clear to the president that the proposed reinterpretation of the LGIM would undermine the financial framework that had allowed the Ambatovy project to go ahead. It was in no one's interest that the company be put in a position where it was forced to default on its debts. It certainly was not in Madagascar's interests that international lending institutions would see the country as a serious risk for future investment.

This was the main message we had to deliver when we drove down the avenue of the leafless baobabs toward the Ivaoloha palace that July morning in 2012. Having seen to our surprise the grandiose banners bearing Rajoelina's photographic portrait, we were ushered into an adjacent hall where once again Rajoelina was joined by his finance minister and several other officials. This was hardly the relatively placid encounter we had enjoyed on our previous *démarche* a year before. Our greater number did not apparently make our case more compelling. For most of the meeting, Rajoelina ceded the floor to Minister Héry (given the length of his surname, the use of his given name was generally accepted). Héry expounded at length on his interpretation of the royalty law and on the Malagasy people's efforts to win just recompense for the exploitation of their resources. All governments need revenues, and resource royalties for the extraction of finite resources are a just and appropriate source. For developing countries with limited capacity to generate income and consumption taxes, royalties are always a tempting source. However, the terms of financing the Ambatovy project and the income that would be shared with government had been agreed upon when the project was initiated. Trying to change those terms when the project was about to get underway was folly. Projects which in time succeed and surpass revenue expectations can anticipate pressures from government to share more of the revenues. To try to impose new terms at the outset hampers a project's success and scares away future investors.

Yet Héry and Rajoelina appeared untroubled. We won no clear commitment by the end of the meeting that they were willing to withdraw the proposed new tax framework. Ambatovy's operating licence was once more in abeyance. And shortly thereafter, adding to the company's predicament, Ambatovy received once again – and this time in a formal letter – the request for a $75 million payment, this time characterized as a deposit to an environmental protection fund, to mitigate against any industrial accidents. Ambatovy pointed out that the company was already obliged to keep aside three months of expenditures amounting to $90 million to cover such accidents and was further required to hold insurance of $150 million during the start-up and $250 million during the operations phases of the project.

I wish I could describe our visit to the Ivaoloha palace as the crucial intervention that convinced Rajoelina to relent in his efforts to squeeze more money from Ambatovy. Unfortunately, the silence following that intervention, offered no evidence that we had had an effect. But Rajoelina eventually did yield. Ambatovy was the largest single investment in a country desperate for development. Madagascar needed international support for the coming elections and the EU countries, which would help finance them, were also among the projects biggest financial backers. Whatever were the considerations that went into the decision, some months after the *démarche*, Ambatovy received the permit to proceed under the original taxation terms. Before I left my southern African assignment, Ambatovy was still fighting the government over the VAT issue, but the mine and the refinery had started production.

It was a celebratory occasion when I visited Madagascar in March 2013. During the previous two years, the high commission had worked to recruit and then win approval from Madagascar authorities for the appointment of an honorary consul. The candidate we found was a joint Malagasy and Canadian citizen, Maggie Leong, who held a Canadian degree in transport economics, had once worked for Aéroports de Montréal and who had returned to Madagascar where she helped her parents operate an inland resort hotel. I was accompanied by Jean Sénécal, the chief mission administrative officer, Monique Kemp, and Cathy Bruno, the consular staff. Our principal objective was to introduce Leong to senior contacts in Tana and hold a cocktail reception in her honour. The reception was at the Hotel Colbert on the palace square, a popular destination for business and government travellers as well as many of the capital's elite. We were pleased to have in attendance the Malagasy government's chief protocol officer, senior officials of the foreign ministry, as well as the many diplomatic contacts with whom I had worked so closely for nearly four years. As the evening wound down after I said good-bye to our guests, the high commission staff and Leong repaired to the balcony off the reception hall and enjoyed some quiet conversation in the late summer air.

"La crise" was not over. The elections had not yet been held. Full diplomatic relations had not been restored. Yet Canada's relations with Madagascar were on a better footing and we were on the path to providing more ample support to our consular and commercial interests in the country. There was a sense of accomplishment and the feeling that we had indeed started to open the door on what was going to be a better chapter in Canada-Malagasy relations. Bilateral relations lie at the heart of the diplomatic profession and though the phrase sounds abstract, its content is not. Behind it are people: Malagasies and Canadians trying to make better lives for themselves and each other.

When completing a pre-determined foreign assignment, diplomats are usually aware that, just as they jumped into the waters mid-stream, so do they leave. They have contributed to, and sometimes completed, some important tasks. But often these affairs continue, only partly resolved, or sometimes, regrettably, further confounded.

After leaving Madagascar, I was able to watch as most of my work there continued to progress. The Canadians falsely implicated in the suspicious bombings were allowed to leave. The health and safety inspector under investigation was safely back in Canada. Successful democratic elections were indeed held, and although Canada did not provide any electoral assistance, the endorsement of the vote by independent electoral observers did allow high commissioner Gaston Barban to present his credentials. Ambatovy went into full production, and generally performed well, despite skirmishes with a new, democratically elected regime, headed by former finance minister and president, Héry Rajaonarimampianina.[5]

11

Virtuous New World (2014–2016)

An ill-defined sense of disorientation, then an unmistakeable trembling, followed by a vigorous rocking and swaying. My wife Suzanne and I were sitting at our kitchen table. The motion swelled, subsided and swelled again, accompanied this time by a shuddering. It seemed a wall might break, the ceiling crack or the floor give way. The combined and contradictory motions of swaying and pulsing, the sliding back and forth, continued in intensity until – after several minutes – all gave way to a vestigial wave motion at our feet.

It was September 16, 2015, and we had just experienced an earthquake of 8.3 magnitude on the Richter scale – a major tremor. We were at home in our apartment on the 13th floor of a 15-storey apartment in the *comuna*, or municipality, of Las Condes in Santiago de Chile.

The earthquake was the most powerful of what became an unpredictable series. Several strong *réplicas*, or after-shocks, followed that evening, and during the next day in my office on the 12th floor of Santiago's unfortunately named World Trade Center, where I was the Canadian Embassy's senior trade commissioner, great jolts from below continued to rattle through the giant twin-towered, 20-storey structure.

That we were at work the day after the first major shock, and during aftershocks that registered in the 6 and 7 Richter ranges, testified to Chile's readiness for such events, and especially to the strength of its building codes, set so that high-rise structures could reliably withstand these literally earthshaking events. In the embassy, porcelain hinges set at intervals along the interior walls had shattered to partly absorb the energy of the shocks, and expansion and contraction joints in the elevator foyer had allowed the building's adjoining towers to sway independently, leaving a gap in the floor through which you could now peer into the basement.

Thanks to these and other structural safeguards, the building was still standing, with minor damage.

The quake did claim its victims. Its epicenter had been near the town of Illapel about 120 kilometres northwest of Santiago. Its source had been another sudden thrust of the Pacific Ocean's Nazca tectonic plate under the South American continent. Fifteen deaths were reported. Some 30,000 people were left temporarily homeless. A tsunami struck the shoreline of the coastal cities of Coquimbo and La Serena, destroying harbour works and beach-front restaurants. Yet given the vast power involved, the damage was relatively limited and our life and work in Santiago was little affected. As many Chileans do, we would become accustomed, even blasé, to these events, which would strike frequently, though at irregular intervals.

My responsibility as senior trade commissioner was to a manage a team of Chilean and Canadian officers charged with connecting Canadian companies with new markets in one of the most business-oriented South American countries. The defence and strengthening of Canada's international security and the promotion of our commercial interests abroad represent the key priorities of Canada's foreign policy. Only the protection of individual Canadian citizens from hazards abroad will at times supplant them. The evacuations of Canadians from Lebanon during civil conflict there in 2006, and the efforts to stop the SARS virus from entering Canada in 2003 are instances when, in my experience, the department's focus on harm reduction pushed our more usual diplomatic and commercial concerns aside.

But crises or no, Global Affairs' ongoing goal of keeping doors open for Canadian trade and investment abroad is always on the menu. It is the day-to-day work of Canada's Trade Commissioner Service, a network of more than 1000 trade specialists working in Canada's more than 160 embassies and consulates abroad. In the context of the ongoing efforts to further trade liberalization which characterized my nearly 30 years in the department, the trade commissioners are the foot soldiers that put policy into practice. Having won market access, we want to use it. Our team of trade commissioners in Santiago was recognized as one of the best in the network.

I knew before arrival that Chile was already well-trodden ground for Canadian business. Canada and Chile had a free trade agreement of nearly

20 years' duration and close to $3 billion in two-way trade. Even more significantly, Canadian firms had an accumulated investment of nearly $18 billion in Chilean electrical utilities, toll highways, sanitation works, mines, banking and industrial production. Canadian companies were number one among foreign investors in mining and third in the Chilean economy overall.

The attraction of Canadian firms to Chile is indeed linked to the country's proclivity for terrestrial disasters, including not just frequent earthquakes, but volcanoes and floods and threatening tides. The instability of Chile's physical foundations, shaken by great tectonic movements exposing once hidden rock structures and filling underground caverns with superhot magma, made the country, through countless millennia, a bountiful receptacle of rich ores and mineral wealth.

Canadian firms have been confident of the strength of the Chilean economy since the return to democracy in 1990, after 17 years of the notorious dictatorship of Augusto Pinochet. Chile followed policies of open markets, business freedom, fiscal discipline and the rule of law since that time, and Canadian investors were keen to take advantage of the consequent opportunities.

The priorities that I pursued as the embassy's trade program manager were to maintain and enhance both the pace of Canadian exports to Chile and build the policy framework in which that trade took place.

The timing was not altogether propitious. Chile had weathered well the international financial crisis of 2008 to 2009, and after this sharp economic contraction, the economy bounced back fuelled by strong international demand for minerals, particularly for Chile's most important metal, copper. This was largely based on the massive appetite of a rapidly growing China. But by 2014 the so-called commodities super-cycle ebbed, and the Chinese economy slowed substantially. The impact was marked, and growth slowed to an insipid rate of less than two per cent annually. This decline corresponded almost exactly with the return to power of President Michelle Bachelet in March 2014. Bachelet led the centre-left coalition that had governed Chile since the democratic restoration, save for one four-year presidential term for the country's centre-right coalition between 2010 and 2014.

Several months into Bachelet's second term (she had also been president from 2006 to 2010) a narrative emerged among the Chilean business class that the decelerating economy was primarily the government's fault. A major reform agenda and implementation of new regulatory measures had brought uncertainty. The government's efforts to enforce compliance with increasingly important and complex environmental regulations had become incoherent, the critics said. Neither officials nor companies were certain how regulatory processes were supposed to work. Regional and national officials, although ostensibly part of the same bureaucratic structure in the highly centralized Chilean state, would make different and conflicting decisions according to distinct and uncertain schedules. Regulatory agencies would also make judgements, which courts would later nullify; so, government institutions were feuding among themselves. The confusion was compounded by the Bachelet government's decision to adopt as domestic law Convention 169 of the International Labor Organization (ILO), a United Nations body, in which the government agreed that no major project – be it mine, dam, electrical grid extension – be approved without aboriginal communities' "free, prior and informed consent."

The business critique went further. The government was also implementing a major business tax reform that, through transferring a portion of companies' tax burdens to the personal accounts of their beneficial owners, effectively reduced the companies' ability to re-invest profits. Chile's rate of investment was falling, thus impeding economic expansion. A new labor relations law had been approved which – if not as strong as legislation in most North American and European jurisdictions – gave more power to labor unions. To these specifically business-related issues, conservative commentators added the launch of constitutional reform, fearing that the government planned to abridge property rights. All of this, businesses were saying, had contributed to an uncertain economic and social environment that was compromising growth. They likened this to the government's taking a bulldozer to Chile's economic success. This analogy took inspiration from the unfortunate assertion of a senior congressman in Bachelet's coalition that the government would take a backhoe to the too-timid reforms of the earlier post-Pinochet governments.[1]

Hermann von Mühlenbrock was the president of one of Chile's most powerful business organizations, SOFOFA, or Sociedad de Fomento

Fabril, which represents the country's manufacturers. On November 5, 2014, I witnessed the rather extraordinary spectacle of his delivering a startlingly audacious public chiding to President Bachelet. SOFOFA is one of numerous Chilean business organizations that represent the range of the country's economic sectors. Each hosts an annual dinner where it is generally expected the President and several cabinet colleagues will attend, along with hundreds of association members, government officials and diplomats. That these associations, or *gremios*, can expect such high-level attention is a deep-seated tradition in Chile, and ministers' schedules are arranged to accommodate these almost compulsory events. It's a modern equivalent of corporatism derived from some of the less malevolent strains of fascist theory, which found traction in Chile dating from the 1920s. The notion is that society is ordered not so much around individuals but around the economic groups to which people belong,[2] and politics should be managed accordingly.

While Chilean politicians can expect to hear the *gremios'* leaders' policy observations during these annual dinners, von Mühlenbrock's musings at the Espacio Riesco, a giant convention and trade fair centre in Santiago's north industrial park, were remarkably severe. The physically imposing and white-haired Mühlenbrock, the host of the event, was seated as protocol demands beside the President throughout the dinner. When he finally took the podium, he released a salvo of criticism that blamed President Bachelet for installing a climate of "growing preoccupation and uncertainty," unleashing a public campaign "severely critical of the private sector" and fomenting an "anti-business attitude" that can only impede the country's growth.[3] Throughout his nearly half-hour diatribe, Bachelet sat stone-faced. Then her response was reserved, even muted. "We have always sought dialogue . . . Modern societies know well, and their businesspeople as well . . . how to make changes that in time gain confidence," changes that must continue rather than be abandoned and leave society "to continue to stand still." In the following days, there was no one I spoke to who did not think that von Mühlenbrock had gone too far. Over lunch, the head of one of Chile's mining *gremios* told me that the SOFOFA president had badly hurt his capacity to influence the government in the future. And in fact, a campaign began to unseat von Mühlenbrock, which he only managed to fend off by a narrow margin in an election the following year. Bachelet, breaking long tradition, did not appear at the next annual dinner.

Canadian companies in Chile shared to various degrees these critical attitudes toward the government. Many of their Chilean managers were members of the same business and social class and shared similar attitudes and assumptions. As foreign investors, however, most of the firms would exercise great caution in their public pronouncements, understanding at any time, they may need to make representations to senior officials or ministers in pursuit of their corporate interests. Companies, of course, paid close attention to Chile's regulatory regime, and for the most part sought to engage the government on issues that were directly relevant to them and the development of their projects. To develop a better understanding among the companies and to better position the Canadian embassy to assist them, if necessary, the Canadian Ambassador, Patricia Fuller, began to convene regular meetings at the embassy of the top Canadian mining companies. Fuller was a career diplomat with an extensive background in economics, strongly dedicated to maintaining Canada's profile in Chile and advancing Canada's interests.

The modern mining industry has evolved in recent years. Although its public image suffers from the perception that its projects inevitably despoil the environment and destroy communities, many of the industry's biggest firms see the incorporation of environmental and social concerns as vital to their business models. This was brought very much to my attention when, in preparation for my posting in Chile, I visited the offices in Ottawa of the Mining Association of Canada (MAC) to learn how they support their members in foreign markets. It was a revelation to me at the time that the MAC had developed guidelines of best practices under the title *Toward Sustainable Mining*, guidelines with which it requires that all member companies comply in their Canadian operations. They are urged to do so abroad as well. Far from this being a public relations gloss, the MAC has established a process whereby auditors review compliance and report when companies fall short. As explained to me by Rick Meyers, MAC's vice-president of technical and northern affairs at the time, the risks to multi-billion investments that damage the environment and harm communities is so significant that high standards are not just an option;

they are a must. The purchase of "social licence" is in fact an integral cost in any major project.

Clearly guidelines, and their regular enforcement, are no guarantee against accident or neglect. Negative public impressions of mining are supported by plenty of evidence. On the day I spoke to Meyers in Ottawa, he was dealing with a flood of reporters' calls over the collapse of Imperial Metals' large tailings dam at the Mount Polley project in northeastern British Columbia. Imperial Metals is a MAC member and therefore a signatory of *Towards Sustainable Mining*. Such accidents are rare. But particularly pertinent to Chile, the Canadian mining company Barrick, one of the world's largest gold miners, had become the *bête noire* of Chile's environmental movement. Works under construction at its prospective multi-billion-dollar Pascua Lama gold mine in Chile's high Andes washed away into local rivers after an unusual high-altitude rainfall. The company had failed to install structures that would have prevented the damage. Barrick admitted that the accident was the company's fault, for not having sequenced its works properly under environmental regulations specifically to avoid damage caused by rare, but possible, Andean rains.

So, in the context of the industry's always vulnerable image on the one hand and its shared vision of "corporate social responsibility" (CSR) on the other, the Chilean country managers of Barrick, Goldcorp, Lundin, Kinross, KGHM and Yamana Gold – the largest Canadian miners in Chile – would gather in the embassy boardroom on a roughly monthly basis at Ambassador Fuller's invitation to review the Chilean mining scene. All the companies were making special efforts to integrate communities in their project planning and seeking to ensure that benefits would be achieved locally. The mantra for all of them was early engagement in consultations to win broad-based community support. And once begun, the importance of patience and perseverance until arriving at a positive consensus. Some companies had established specific programs, such as Lundin's special foundation for community improvement projects in Tierra Amarillo, or Teck's establishment of a project to increase the participation of women in mining. But the embassy round tables were not just to highlight their CSR initiatives, they also served as sounding boards for the challenges of the Chilean regulatory process.

During the round table discussions, it was evident that the Canadian companies were not "feeling the love" from the government despite their efforts to be good corporate citizens. During one session with Chile's then-environment minister Pablo Badenier, the executives let their frustration show. One complained of having to obtain "283 permits," and another of having to submit the same information to two or three levels of government. Still another complained of the "enormous cost" in both time and money. The well-publicized travails of Goldcorp's El Morro project put the companies' quandary into sharp relief. Chile's Supreme Court in October 2014 over-turned the Chilean environmental commission's approval of the company's planned a $4.5 billion investment[4] in an Atacama region copper mine. The reason? The Chilean commission for Indigenous development had not conducted an adequate consultation process. The essence of the court's judgement did not relate to any failing of the company, but rather the fault lay with Chile's own authorities as they had failed to manage, sequence and fulfill their own regulatory requirements.

All the Canadian companies who sat at the round table had encountered incoherence in the approval process and had become deeply frustrated that their efforts to invest billions in the Chilean economy during a period of generally slow growth were being thwarted.

Ambassador Fuller suggested to the minister that the answer to the companies' grievances should be: "one project-one review." And she pressed this view subsequently on several other Chilean cabinet ministers, including those responsible for mining, the economy, industry, social development and the treasury. She would refer, during these meetings to a Canadian process to expedite large-project approvals, known as the major projects management office (MPMO) housed in Natural Resources Canada. The reference to the Canadian domestic initiative sparked interest among the Chilean authorities and a wish to know more. The ambassador decided then to have the embassy invite a representative of the MPMO to visit Santiago to make a presentation on how the Canadian process worked.

Given the difficulty that Canada has had in recent years finalizing approvals for major projects, one might question the value of promoting the Canadian experience. After all, several oil pipelines and liquefied natural gas plants – to name just these – have languished as blueprints while their proponents have been unable to negotiate their way past the obstacles of provincial and first nations approvals, let alone the federal government's own energy and environmental hurdles. That said, the concept of the MPMO and its principle of close tracking of projects through the variety of regulatory hoops and the disciplined imposition of a "bring-forward" schedule had much to recommend it.

We convened the seminar on the MPMO in Club 50, an event centre in the heart of Santiago's modern business district. The club is in an ultra-modern tower at the edge of the still-cobblestoned circle of El Golf, which connects the hard-driving, all business avenue of Apoquindo with Isadora Goyenechea, the more relaxed boulevard of restaurants and high-end shops. Our presenter was Jim Clarke, the MPMO's executive director, a Canadian civil servant of lean physique and friendly demeanour who evinced a singular commitment to his office's mandate, which was, essentially, "to get things done." The crowd comprised top government officials, including Luis Felipe Céspedes, minister of industry, and the undersecretary of mining, Ignacio Moreno, and businesspeople, including the soon to be president of the Chilean mining association, Diego Hernandez. Also, in attendance, were some of Chile's top regulators including representatives of the environmental evaluation commission and the mineral and geological service.

The response to this event exceeded our expectations. In the following weeks, the Chilean government established a high-level, regulatory monitoring committee, comprising senior economic ministers reporting directly to then-Treasury Minister Rodrigo Valdés. And gradually some of the projects that had been waiting in the wings began to wend their way through the system of permits and approvals. It was not that the government was short-circuiting the regulatory regime. Rather, it was riding herd on the various processes to ensure they were undertaken in appropriate sequence and completed in a timely manner, without sacrificing due diligence. From 2015 to 2017, major projects for Canadian major mining companies Teck and Lundin and smaller Canadian players such as Los Andes Copper, among others, obtained important certificates allowing them to move ahead. These results stemmed at least in part from the Canadian embassy's initiative. They represented clear achievements that were significant examples of the value of economic diplomacy.

During the introduction of an embassy-sponsored seminar on mines tailings management, Alberto Salas, the head of Chile's equivalent of the Canadian Chamber of Commerce (*Confederación de la Producción y del Comercio*) made the following observation: "Chile's mines are among the largest producers of minerals in the world. They are even larger producers of mine tailings." The truth of this is obvious, but it is brought home on any visit to any mine anywhere. It is particularly so when it is the world's largest copper mine, El Teniente, that had been in operation since 1904.

The mine is located at about 2,300 metres in the Andes about 120 kilometres southeast of Santiago. The continuous production of copper ore for more than a century has resulted in the accumulation of vast tailings deposits that cover the bottoms of two adjacent valleys, Cauquenes and Colihues. Despite its long history of copper production, Chile's remaining reserves of the still-indispensable industrial mineral are immense. But many of these reserves are in Chile's central zone of mediterranean climate and verdant agriculture, where most of Chile's population lives. Much of Chile's current mining is done in the arid desert zones, which have ecological challenges of their own, but not the level of impact that would accompany mining in the central zone. El Teniente is just such a mine, and the work done here needs to inform future developments in this region.

One spring morning in 2017, I joined several interested industry and embassy observers in traveling to a Canadian-owned project near El Teniente that, for more than a decade, has been mining the tailings themselves to extract copper left behind. The concentrations in the historical deposits are high due to the less efficient extraction processes used in the past, but even the fresh tailings there contained a substantial copper residue. Vancouver-based Amerigo Resources is the owner and operator of the facility, in which old tailings, a thick grey sludge, are washed away by high-pressure hoses into a canal that flows into a series of separation tanks in which copper is effectively floated away or skimmed from the surface. Since the use of chemicals is minimal, there is no contamination of the watershed. Of course, the "used" tailings are then returned to their original impoundments, and little has been done to reduce the volumes significantly. Despite improving the economic efficiency of the mine, the material remains a challenge for present and future generations.

Chile is acutely aware of these challenges and a consortium of business, government and academia, styling itself *Valor Minero*, or Mining Value, has been established to tackle these issues. But the scale of hardrock mining is such that tailings will remain a perpetual legacy and setting the boundary between the original contours of the Andean valleys and the altered post-mining landscape will always be a difficult task for governments, industry and communities.

I became more directly acquainted with these issues when the town of Putaendo (population about 1,000) attempted to implicate the Canadian embassy in a controversy around a local mining project. Canadian-owned Los Andes Copper was undertaking a drilling program to prove the extent and concentration of a copper ore body near the town. Putaendo is on a tributary of the Aconcagua River, some 100 kilometres north of Santiago near the town of Los Andes, in the heart of one of Chile's northernmost wine regions. A vocal group of local activists was attempting to raise opposition to the project, accusing it of not having received regulatory authority for its drilling program. Among their concerns was that the waters to be drawn from the river might reduce the quantities available for agricultural irrigation and be contaminated by drilling chemicals. They had drawn attention to its Canadian ownership and had called for a meeting with the embassy to raise their concerns. There was the implication that Canada was condoning irresponsible resource exploitation. The opponents hoped that the embassy would be embarrassed into condemning the company's behaviour as a violation of Canadian values supporting corporate social responsibility. Ambassador Marcel Lebleu (who had recently replaced Ambassador Fuller) was reluctant to give the activists an increased profile. But he agreed it would be damaging if we were accused of refusing to meet. The solution was that *he* would not meet the activists, but that I would. Should the encounter go awry, the ambassador would still have his own reputation unblemished and might be able to mitigate damage.

On the appointed day, Putaendo Mayor (or *alcalde*) Guillermo Reyes came to my office accompanied by a spokesperson for the activists, who had organized themselves under the banner *Putaendo Resiste* (Putaendo Resists). I was joined by our trade section's expert on corporate social responsibility, Margot Edwards, a Canadian who had lived in Chile for many years and was recognized for her knowledge and tact. The activist argued that Los Andes Copper was not abiding by drilling regulations, was affecting water flows in the river and the development was detrimental to local agriculture. We had informed ourselves in advance about the regulatory status of the project. The company seemed to be complying with the law. There was a case currently before the courts on one issue, but it was our view that the Chilean legal process must be allowed to work. At one point I asked – all technicalities aside – whether the group desired that the project not be allowed to go ahead, simply because they didn't want a mining project in their town. The mayor answered without equivocation that that was exactly his position.

To our relief, Mayor Reyes and the activists' representative did not try to capitalize on the meeting to create negative publicity. The mayor mentioned the meeting in a press release but made no accusations. We had made a judgement call to meet him and it appeared to have paid off.

The future of the Putaendo project was uncertain. Los Andes Copper's prospecting confirmed that the ore body is of high grade and contained some 25 years of production. Nonetheless many in the community remained concerned that should the mine be developed, a local valley, albeit at altitudes higher than the agricultural zone in which the town is located, might alter the mountain landscape forever. There would obviously have to be a trade-off between local jobs and development and impact on the environment, even if the impact was mitigated by the highest standards envisioned in "towards sustainable mining."

✷ ✷ ✷

Among Latin American countries, Chile is much admired for its adherence to the rule of law. It is an important feature of its attractiveness as an investment destination. However, the country's reputation in this regard was cast in a rather dubious light with the eruption in 2014 of a political financing scandal that swept up nearly all the countries' political parties. The agent in this affair was the renowned Chilean non-metallic mining company SQM (Sociedad Quimica y Minera de Chile), a producer of potassium and nitrates, key fertilizer components, and lithium, the highly prized material that powers electric vehicle batteries. SQM mines deposits in northern Chile from leases that are granted by the state, and it was revealed that for several years running, the company had been hedging its bets, relative to possible future political transitions, by systematic secret contributions to virtually all major political parties. The paymaster was Patricio Contesse, the company's executive director, and the "under-the-table" payments were carried out apparently under his sole discretion – or at least without any formal directive from SQM's board of directors.

This matter would normally be of interest to the Canadian embassy. It is one of the embassy's roles to report important political developments to headquarters in Ottawa. However, this case was particularly relevant since one of SQM's controlling shareholders was Potash Corporation of Saskatchewan (PCS), giving rise to the concern that a major Canadian investor might be implicated. The danger to its reputation was not at all lost on PCS.

For Canadian trade commissioners to offer services to Canadian companies – especially if it might involve communication with local governments – it is imperative to know that the companies' practices comply with ethical standards. Specifically, companies since 2014 have been asked – when they seek the aid of the Trade Commissioner Service – to sign declarations that they have not been involved in such activity as offering bribes.

PCS had a 32 per cent ownership stake in SQM. There was an agreement with the other controlling shareholder Juan Ponce Lerou that neither owner would acquire a greater share of the firm than the other – guaranteeing a continuing deadlock in beneficial ownership. What made the SQM political funding scandal particularly radioactive was that Ponce was the ex-son-in-law of the late Chilean dictator Augusto Pinochet, an unsavory connection for much of the Chilean public, as well as for Bachelet's governing coalition.

As senior trade commissioner, I needed to get PCS's side of the story. From his office in Saskatoon, Wayne Brownlee, the executive vice-president, explained that the company had been caught off-guard and had not only been offended by the political payouts, which, he said, none of PCS's representatives on the board had been informed of, but worried also about possible legal problems that could descend on the company's directors from – especially – the United States Securities and Exchange

Commission (SEC). The mechanism of Contesse's clandestine political donations was through his solicitation of "consulting" reports from individuals associated with one or other of the main political parties. Many of these reports contained little original content, and at times were merely compendia of material gleaned from the internet. The "authors" were paid for these reports, and the receipts would be recycled into political campaigns. Among prominent practitioners of this art was Rodrigo Peñailillo, one of Bachelet's senior organizers for her 2013 presidential election campaign and later her minister of the interior.

Following the first of the revelations, PCS's reaction was rapid. They advised the board of directors that they were withdrawing their three members from the eight-person board and they insisted on Contesse's departure. That Contesse had been able to carry out this scheme – which at one point was said to have disbursed more than $20 million (Cdn) – brought into question the adequacy of SQM's corporate governance. So, during the formal absence of PCS directors on the board, PCS negotiated a complete overhaul that brought in a new set of directors, that included, for PCS's representation, three senior executives of PCS itself. Although US authorities did eventually impose a heavy fine on SQM that materially affected the company's share value, none of the directors, except Contesse, faced legal prosecution.

When I first arrived in Chile, I was welcomed by a handover note written by my predecessor, Peter Furesz. He said I was about to take on the best job in the entire trade commissioner service. He had good reason to say that. There are few countries where Canada's business interests are as prominent as they are in Chile. I was to learn in practice that my job was not only to help Canadian companies sell their goods and services, but also to help build an appreciation that industry could and would respect and foster the social and environmental conditions so important to the Chilean government and its people. Even when bound to finding profits for their shareholders, it was a genuinely held conviction that modern business – and emphatically the mining industry – could operate successfully in a virtuous new world quite at odds with its exploitive reputation of old.

Beyond that nuanced role of enhanced commercial promotion, as senior trade commissioner I also needed to work with Chilean colleagues to promote the policy rules that govern trade and investment within the broader international policy framework. That framework, which I have noted throughout this memoir, was founded on an international consensus generally accepted by the member nations of the WTO. But despite having always been the subject of some criticism from those opposed to "neo-liberal globalization," it was soon to come under sudden and much more profound attack with the unexpected election victory of US Republican presidential candidate Donald Trump. Trump's surprising arrival in the White House, a metaphorical earthquake of a Richter scale rivalling the physical one that had shaken us in our Santiago apartment, was high among the conditions that would drive a reboot of the embassy's trade policy initiatives in my final year in Chile.

12

Chile and the Progressive Trade Agenda (2017)

Chileans will often remind visitors that their country was once known as *finis terrae,* the end of the earth. Its northern deserts, the Andes *cordillera* and the inhospitable Cape Horn seas always challenged would-be visitors. But far from being a lost corner of the world, Chile was during my tenure in the country, a full-fledged member of the network of international trade agreements that regulated the globalized world. Chile's physical isolation is a good part of the reason its governments of both right and left adopted such openness to world commerce.

In the early 2010s, the international consensus about the value of ever-liberalizing world commerce had reached its high-water mark. A rising tide of populist and nationalist opposition to this model, greatly under-estimated even at that late stage, had not yet breached the three-decade-long bulwarks of conventional wisdom. Although the Doha round of World Trade Organization talks had foundered, a substitute path to wider liberalization had been charted through the negotiations for the TransPacific Partnership (TPP) involving the United States, Japan, Australia, New Zealand, Mexico, Singapore, Brunei, Malaysia, Peru, Vietnam, Canada and Chile. The negotiations brought together countries representing about 800 million consumers and roughly 36 per cent of the world's GDP. Negotiators, conscious of criticisms that previous trade agreements had side-lined concerns about social justice in favour of a con-centration on economic growth, were negotiating additional provisions on co-operation and capacity-building, development, and transparency and anti-corruption. As well, in keeping with changes that had entered world markets two decades earlier, an article on e-commerce was incorporated.

Negotiators proclaimed the TPP a truly modern agreement that established "a gold standard" for such pacts.

For Canada, which had a 20-year-old bilateral trade agreement with Chile, the TPP would enhance an already-strong trade policy framework that we were in the process of updating. Those updates to a series of technical provisions covering sanitary and phytosanitary measures related to food safety; technical barriers to trade such as incompatible regulations; and government procurement provisions were already underway under the government of Stephen Harper. But with the election of Justin Trudeau in October 2015, the new government saw the talks as a way to introduce some ideas from what it called a progressive trade agenda.

From the point of view of the world trade agenda of ever-expanding markets and freer trade in goods and services all seemed to be following the prescribed trajectory. Until that accepted consensus was suddenly challenged by the emergence of long-suppressed populist political forces in the United States and Europe, which disdained the forces of globalization and which found expression in the election of Donald Trump, and in Britain's ill-fated referendum on Brexit, its proposed exit from the European Union.

The Canadian Embassy in Chile had long been awaiting a "high-level" visitor to underline how much we valued our relationship with Chile; that we held this enduring and law-abiding democracy and business-friendly market in high regard; and we wanted to keep moving forward on a mutually beneficial and amiable trajectory.

A problem – ironically – was that there was little to complain about in our official relations. Canada had recently done away with the requirement that Chileans obtain visas before travelling to Canada, a move welcomed by individual tourists, families, and businesses in both countries. Some Chilean winemakers were pressing the Ontario government for not giving sufficient or prominent shelf space in provincial liquor stores. But this matter was wending its way through a formal dispute settlement process. Pressed to name an outstanding "irritant," we managed to refer only to Chile's reluctance to accept imports of Canadian salmonid eggs for breeding on fish farms. Not the stuff of headlines. With little need for care and maintenance, there were few practical reasons for statesmen to meet, or for officials to spend the hours, days, and weeks necessary to organize a logistically complicated official visit, when more pressing problems elsewhere in the world made greater claims on their time.

Nonetheless, the Chilean foreign ministry was making it clear that they would more than welcome a visit, especially from a representative of the recently elected Justin Trudeau government, to burnish – for its domestic audience – the "progressive" credentials both countries shared. At the very least, the two countries should celebrate the 20th anniversary of the Canada-Chile Free Trade Agreement. An unstated motive for the Chileans was that the beleaguered Bachelet government could try to polish its battered reputation before the end of its scheduled term in office in the hope it would assist the new leader of Bachelet's political coalition in the election to come.

As with so much else in that period, it was the unlikely election of US President Donald Trump and his bellicose and disruptive trade agenda that finally kicked our visit planning into high gear. Trump's decision to withdraw from the TPP prompted an effort of TPP members to try to save the furniture by negotiating a deal that did not include the United States. It was the first proposal of such a rescue that brought a commitment from our headquarters to dispatch then-International Trade Minister François-Phillippe Champagne to Santiago.

Canada had been a somewhat hesitant partner in the TPP. As with the NAFTA more than 20 years before, the Liberals were suffering a bout of bad conscience in endorsing a proposed trade agreement that a previous Conservative government had negotiated and over which the Liberals had cast doubt. There were worries from some sectors, including among them the auto, supplied-managed dairy and poultry, and generic pharmaceutical sectors. There were also the perennial issues of the environment, gender equity, and labour standards brought forward by "civil society" organizations. The Liberals' strategy to respond to these concerns was first to run longwinded consultations at the end of which it was expected they might agree to proceed, if they were able to introduce features of a "progressive trade agenda" in further negotiations.

When Donald Trump announced that the United States would withdraw from the TPP, the immediate reaction of many was that the deal was dead. The US market was so important for each national participant that none would see any advantage without Washington's membership. In fact, under the agreement's terms, without the US economy the requisite level of combined GDP would fall short of the threshold necessary for ratification. My inquiries to our geographic desk and TPP negotiators were met by the immediate response that this arduously negotiated accord had met the fate of the proverbial Monty Python parrot (That being: It is deceased, demised, passed on, no more).

This fatalism was not shared by other TPP members, however. Chile, through statements issued by the top trade official of the foreign ministry's economic directorate (DIRECON), Paulina Nazal, broached the possibility that the TPP could be kept alive even without US participation. Nazal first raised this idea during the Asia Pacific Economic Cooperation (APEC) Summit in Lima, Peru, in late November 2016, suggesting resuscitation in a modified form. To bring it more openly to the table, Chile invited the TPP members, as well as China and South Korea, to attend a "high-level dialogue on the integration initiatives in the Asia-Pacific region" in the resort city of Viña del Mar, on March 14 and 15, 2017.

Enter Champagne, who had recently replaced Chrystia Freeland as trade minister, in a cabinet shuffle, in which Freeland moved on to the foreign ministry. Views were shifting on a TPP revival as Chile coaxed reconsideration. Although the invitation for Canada to attend the dialogue had moved desultorily through several political and bureaucratic filters before reaching Champagne's office, the minister quickly accepted it. He arrived in Chile on March 13. Brimming with enthusiasm as Canada's "top salesman" – as he described himself – he was a compact force of charm and positivity. Champagne was like an actor who is always "on." His entrances were rapid, and he sought to command his stage. Although he is at the low end of five feet something, he was an unmistakeable presence. He exhibited a well-honed confidence and immediately struck up conversations that were pleasant but nonetheless "on message." He was a political pupil of prime minster Jean Chrétien in his Shawinigan riding before launching a career in international business. If not as folksy as Chrétien, he was as direct and uncomplicated. A meeting with embassy staff was arranged for his arrival.

"We are very proud of what the Trade Commissioner Service does," he said to me on our being introduced. "Your work around the world is excellent. You are providing Canadians with a truly vital service to advance

Canada's interests." Rote perhaps, but certainly appreciated by any trade commissioner who believes in his or her work, as most do.

The key event organized for Champagne by the embassy before the Viña del Mar "international dialogue" was a business lunch at the Club 50. We had arranged to commemorate the 20th anniversary of the Canada-Chile Free Trade Agreement and had specially produced for the occasion a video in which Chrétien, whose government negotiated the deal, would offer a few words of welcome. The former prime minister delivered his recorded remarks in his typically plain-spoken style and extended his regards to former Chilean president Eduardo Frei Ruiz-Tagle, the leader who signed the original deal, and who was seated with Champagne at the head table.

Champagne's speech was replete with the new "progressive trade" gospel: "We have in Chile a partner committed to a rules-based, fair trading environment and a progressive and open trade agenda . . . When nations trade together, good things happen for our people, and that is ultimately our primary objective: making trade work for people . . . (But) we need to do everything we can to ensure that the benefits of trade are more widely and equitably shared." In these remarks could be heard the echo of the Lloyd Axworthy's "human security agenda" revealing a satisfying continuum between Liberal regimes.

We had been working on making improvements to the Canada-Chile agreement since my arrival in Chile in 2014. One of the first functions Suzanne and I organized, in our apartment in Las Condes, was a reception that brought together Canadian and Chilean negotiators who were working on modifications of the chapter on technical barriers to trade. The subject sounds dry but it's an important feature of modern trade agreements. Regulations between countries are different but may be aimed at achieving the same objective. If officials can agree, for example, that each side's regulations on electrical appliances ensure their safety, then the rules can be recognized as equivalent, and the appliances can be sold in each other's market.

I didn't hear much talk about the substance of the negotiations that evening at our apartment. Instead, it was a chance to connect with many of Chile's trade policy experts, who I would need to work with in the months to come. Among them was Alejandro Buvinic, who would soon be named the head of Chile's equivalent of the Trade Commissioner Service, ProChile. As was so often the case, the party drifted to our apartment's large balcony from which we could see the glimmering lights of "Sanhattan," Santiago's modern business district on one side, and the peaks of the Andes on the other, their glaciers reflecting the sunset glow. The pleasure of the social occasion would pay dividends in our relations with Chilean officials in the months to come.

Throughout my assignment in Chile, negotiators worked on other changes to the trade agreement including chapters on rules of origin and government procurement, as well as the chapter on investor-state dispute settlement. This latter had been added to the agenda by Freeland shortly after she was appointed as trade minister in a clear effort to respond to free trade critics who had consistently and for years inveighed against this provision as it had originally appeared in NAFTA. In fact, I remember quite clearly NAFTA chief negotiator John Weekes telling me of this breakthrough in trade governance, describing it as a major and positive feature to expedite the resolution of investment disputes. The critics, though, said it gave private, foreign companies unusual power to overturn government regulations made for the public good. Hostility toward the NAFTA investor-state chapter in Canada grew in the wake of successful cases brought against Canadian governments by US investors, some yielding substantial settlements that the Canadian government had to pay.

Freeland inherited such a chapter in the talks for Canada-European Union Comprehensive Economic and Trade Agreement (CETA), all but completed by Stephen Harper's Conservative government. Freeland, eager to put the Liberal government's "progressive" stamp on the deal, negotiated modifications that stressed the right of governments to regulate in the public interest. The changes also included a permanent dispute settlement body supposedly more impartial than the ad hoc boards established under NAFTA.

I agreed with headquarters to consult the top Canadian investors in Chile on possible changes to the investor-state chapter. I set out on foot from the embassy to consult the chief executive officers or board chairs whose offices were scattered around the Sanhattan business district. The reaction I got did not surprise me. The relationship between Canada and Chile is rather different than that with many other trade partners, including the US and the EU. Unlike the Canada-US market for example, investment between Canada and Chile is mostly one-way and very much in Canada's favour. While Chilean investment in Canada is relatively small, Canadian investment in Chile is massive, amounting to about $18 billion during my tenure as senior trade commissioner.

Most of the top managers of Canadian businesses in Chile are Chilean nationals, mostly men of conservative tastes, practiced charm and cultivated manners. In some dozen offices in the boardrooms of glass-towered headquarters, these men received me politely. As I explained Canada's wishes on free trade reform, their collective response was one of puzzlement. From their perspective, the investor-state dispute settlement chapter as it stood was a powerful instrument to protect their Canadian owners' interests against any arbitrary and adverse changes in Chilean laws or regulations. In the 20 years of the agreement, the provision had never been used, but they all saw it as a valuable backstop, an insurance policy.

There had in fact been one instance where the Canadian company; Methanex, had been tempted to resort to the dispute settlement provision. The company, whose origin was in the gas fields of Medicine Hat, Alberta, and which operated a large methanol production facility at Punta Arenas in Chile's far south, had been denied supply of natural gas feedstock by Chile's state-owned oil company, Empresa Nacional de Petroleo (ENAP). The failure to meet this contractual obligation had been forced on ENAP by a decision of the Argentine government to suspend all sales of natural gas to neighbouring markets. What gas Chile was able to draw from its own reserves was needed for heating and power in the southernmost, and coldest, part of Chile. Methanex, however, decided not to invoke the dispute settlement mechanism, choosing instead to work with the Chilean government towards a long-term solution. In fact, that solution emerged during my stay in Chile, as ENAP after years of exploration in the Magallanes region, was able to find sufficiently large gas reserves to meet both the region's residential and, to Methanex's satisfaction, industrial needs.

Despite the tendency of Chilean-based Canadian companies to seek to work with, rather than confront, Chilean authorities – as illustrated by the Methanex case – the executives were still baffled that Canada, without any pressure from the Chilean government, would make a voluntary change in the agreement that could reduce their leverage in the Chilean market. This I reported to Ottawa along with my assessment, based on the interviews, that none of the Canadian companies, despite their objection to the change, would be inclined to oppose publicly what Minister Freeland so clearly wanted. However, it was my personal evaluation, that the Canada-Chile agreement was a poorly chosen target on which to display the government's "progressive" trade credentials, as it theoretically impeded Canadian interests without any offsetting advantage. But it was clear that the government's desire to profile the progressive trade agenda took precedence in this case over national self-interest.

I wondered whether any of these executives would raise the issue with Champagne in a series of meetings we arranged before his speech to the Canada-Chile Chamber of Commerce. They did not, preferring to underline, in their polished and diplomatic manner, the harmonious relations they, for the most part, maintained with the Chilean government.

Champagne was still intent on promoting another aspect of the "progressive" agenda, the participation of women in trade. He stressed that his first meeting after landing in Chile had been with top executives of the Canadian mining company Teck, which was running a program, in conjunction with the agency; United Nations Women, to help Indigenous women benefit at the local level from business activity associated with the company's Chilean projects. In his speech to the Chamber, he said: "Teck entered into a US$1 million partnership . . . to promote the empowerment of Indigenous women in the northern regions of Chile. The project seeks to promote capacity building among Indigenous women and address the barriers to their active political and economic participation." "Capacity building," one of the buzzwords of the modern international development professional, means equipping people with the tools and skills to move ahead under their own steam without need for grants, subsidies or other financial supports.

In the weeks leading up to Champagne's visit, we had been in close communication with headquarters over the measures necessary to finally to wrap up the new chapters of the Canada-Chile trade agreement, which we called its "modernization." As his arrival approached, I exchanged numerous secure messages with headquarters colleagues.

All embassies have a secure area called the "vault" which houses their most secure communications equipment. The one in Santiago happened to be particularly frigid, partly due to the need to cool the embassy's computer server, and I was shivering as I composed one morning a secure e-mail to Ottawa summarizing the state-of-play respecting official approval of the new free trade chapters. Ambassador Lebleu dropped by and suggested that I include in my message, a proposal that Ottawa, in keeping with the progressive agenda, consider negotiation of a new chapter on women and trade. He wanted me to advise that such a proposal would likely be accepted by Chile, since our Chilean counterparts had recently negotiated such a pact with the government of Uruguay, the first in any trade agreement.

"I don't think they'll go for it," I said, speaking of our colleagues at headquarters. "The existing chapters have taken long enough as it is. And there are still all the formalities of putting the package through cabinet, and Parliament, and the formal exchange of notes."

I had anticipated headquarters' reaction exactly. In less than 24 hours, we were thanked for the ambassador's suggestion but told that the formal procedures and schedule could not accommodate a completely new chapter.

Apparently, the idea had not been considered serious enough to raise to the level of Champagne's office. When Lebleu, at the Viña del Mar meeting, mentioned the idea to Champagne, the minister's response was instant and enthusiastic. He immediately told his accompanying staff to advise Global Affairs deputy minister Tim Sargent to get the wheels rolling for the negotiation of a "gender and trade" chapter. Lebleu, who liked to push boundaries and challenge traditional ways of doing things, had scored a small triumph.

I had the pleasure of attending the first round of the "women and trade" negotiations, where it became evident a deal would quickly be reached. The talks were led on our side by an experienced trade policy executive, David Usher. The chapter, as first modelled in the Chile-Uruguay deal, did not impose any burdensome requirements. Its primary purpose was to establish a series of regular consultations through a binational committee that would review measures promoting women's involvement in the trade economy. I understand how critics might dismiss the provision as window-dressing, but other side deals have proved productive in the past. The environmental cooperation side agreement of the Canada-Chile free trade deal is a case in point. Since its implementation officials have demonstrated a high level of commitment and pushed practical research on climate change. But these provisions do rely on the goodwill of the partners, and a parallel side deal on labour cooperation had much less to show after years of only desultory activity. It was telling that one of the biggest obstacles to concluding the gender and trade chapter were the objections of Labour Canada, fearing that the consultation process would undermine what they saw as an equivalent process under the labour side deal – but which had seen no results. The "progressive" women's chapter was wrapped up in little more than three months, and it was ready to be announced, along with the rest of the modernized package, during the subsequently organized state visit to Canada of President Bachelet in June 2017.

Champagne's activist trade diplomacy fit the moment. The Valparaíso meeting led ultimately to the re-negotiation of the TPP without the United States, under the name of the Comprehensive and Progressive Agreement for Trans-Pacific Partnership, which entered into force on December 30, 2018. Champagne was no longer in the portfolio, having been moved by Prime Minister Trudeau to Infrastructure Canada in July 2018. In truth, his profile in what has always been a prominent ministry had been eclipsed by Foreign Minister Freeland who had retained the Canada-US negotiations file, which dominated headlines in 2017 and 2018.

Ironically, one of the casualties of the successful talks for a revised NAFTA, the Canada-US-Mexico Trade Agreement, was the investor-state dispute settlement chapter. Despite the effort to make this provision more "progressive" in the Canada-Chile Free Trade Agreement, Canadian negotiators saw fit to accept its elimination in the new NAFTA. This concession to the Trump administration actually answered the prayers of some of Canada's fiercest NAFTA opponents. Seen as a back door to undermine Canadian sovereignty, Chapter 11 was now put out with the trash, with little public lamentation. It lives on however in Canada's agreements with the European Union and Chile.

✳ ✳ ✳

As the southern hemisphere summer began to turn to fall in April 2017, the time for our departure from Chile drew nigh. Although my tenure as senior trade commissioner had coincided with a period of slow economic growth for Chile, there was still no shortage of Canadian firms scouting the market for sales and investment. One of my last appointments was with the head of a major Canadian diversified company exploring new opportunities in energy, infrastructure, and manufacturing. The firm had previous experience in the Chilean market; it had sold its assets in the country to a rival firm several years ago at an advantageous price. It had stayed clear of Chile for several years to comply with its agreement not to compete with the buyer. Now those terms had expired, and it was ready to return to the market.

What was an emerging trend was the arrival of Chinese investors in the Chilean market for the first time. Although China had made strong inroads into other Latin American countries, these tended to be poorer countries eager to accept Chinese capital with few restrictions. Chile's stricter regulatory environment; its attractiveness to a diversity of international investors; and hence little temptation of Chilean authorities to make special concessions to lure investors, had kept Chinese capital at bay. But there were signs that China had begun to recognize that to enter the Chilean market, its firms had to pay competitive prices for available assets. In the months before and after my departure, Chinese companies bought the lion's share of Canadian assets in SQM and the assets of Canadian-owned Brookfield Asset Management in Chile's main electricity trunk line company, Transelec. The tectonic plates of the world economy were starting to shift, and Canadian firms would need to factor in the challenges posed by expanding, more robust and state-supported Chinese enterprises.

My departure from Chile was not just the end of another assignment. It also represented an exit into the final anteroom of my career. That moment my personnel officer Luc Cousineau had mentioned to me 27 years ago was imminent. It had always been my intention to retire shortly after I turned 65. It was time for me to leave room for equally ambitious young officers moving upward through the department's ranks. I advised the department's executive staffing office that I would take my leave in January 2018.

I was amazed, after so many years devoted to pursuit of a set of general organizing principles regarding trade and diplomacy, to see these so readily abandoned by the United States which, since the end of the Second World War and through both Democratic and Republican administrations, had been their most faithful advocate. What had characterized my work at the embassy was a dedication to not only maintain but further enhance the trade policy framework in accordance with a commitment to open markets and free trade. It is clear that countries like Chile have not lost faith in these principles, but could Canada, Chile, and the likeminded countries of the TPP and the EU manage to abide by them in the face of the iconoclasm of the Trump administration, the threat to the EU caused by Brexit and a resurgence of nationalism, and the eruption of public scepticism about the benefits of globalization? Could the old consensus be rescued, or a new one constructed? Would, as Justin Trudeau's Liberals hoped, the progressive trade agenda be enough to persuade doubters that the international trade policy structure is worth saving? Or has its fate been completely taken out of our hands at the start of new era of winner take all, beggar the hindmost?

Epilogue

My career at Global Affairs Canada began in 1990 shortly before air-launched cruise missiles smashed into targets in Baghdad in an internationally televised spectacle of high-tech warfare. It was a violent and inauspicious beginning for what was supposed to be the post-Cold War "new world order." More benignly, the years that followed saw the growth of a broad economic and political consensus around the merits of the rules-based multilateral order.

If the events of the Persian Gulf War were astounding in their day, more striking 26 years later was the almost unbelievable election of Donald Trump to the US presidency on November 4, 2016, setting off a political earthquake in which the accepted precepts of beneficial globalization were thrown into profound doubt, shaken and badly fractured.

In my final months at Global Affairs before my January 2018 retirement, I worked again at the imposing Pearson Building headquarters. I was assigned to a program to help small- and medium-sized Canadian firms take advantage of market access opened by an array of trade agreements signed over the previous three decades. These included the NAFTA, the EU-Canada trade deal, the incipient Trans-Pacific Partnership, the still-extant Uruguay Round agreement to establish the World Trade Organization, and numerous bilateral and regional deals, such as those with the Pacific Alliance countries, including Chile.

Global Affairs' Trade Commissioner Service was one of several federal agencies, government-wide, allied in the "accelerated growth service" which was to equip highly competitive small- and medium-sized firms with greater means for rapid expansion, including enhanced access to new foreign markets. While focused on the very practical details of companies' business plans, it was still impossible to ignore the not-so-distant blows being struck against the Canadian international trade policy edifice that might hobble these companies' chances in years to come.

The NAFTA, which consumed so much labour in my early days at headquarters, was North America's fundamental economic charter. As Trump sought to renegotiate it, once carefully balanced measures became a play chest whose contents were to be tossed about and fiddled with. Trump blamed the NAFTA for many of the United States' economic ills, and his pledge to re-negotiate it was based on crude and narrow economic views. Scorning its features founded on a rules-based approach to international commerce, Trump embarked on a series of arbitrary actions wholly alien to the original spirit of the deal. It was no surprise that his administration announced countervailing and anti-dumping duties against Canadian softwood lumber after the expiry of the 2006 softwood lumber deal. But it was unprecedented that he would impose duties against Canadian aluminum and steel exports on spurious "national security" grounds.

None of these issues – not lumber, nor steel nor aluminum – was resolved in the 2018 revision of NAFTA, the Canada-US-Mexico Trade Agreement. The Trump administration later relented and abandoned the steel and aluminum tariffs, only to re-impose them and again relent on the eve of the 2020 US presidential election.

Canada's communication strategy for the 2018 round differed from the NAFTA strategy for the 1994 agreement. The Trump administration made no secret of its objectives for rolling back original provisions. It was imperative therefore that the Canadian negotiation team be seen to resist these demands. Rather than keeping their own counsel, Canadian negotiators publicly floated compromise solutions, determined to be showing publicly the good faith in which it was trying to negotiate. Among these proposals were, for example, changes to rules of origin on vehicles which were eventually successfully incorporated in the amended deal.

The new agreement cleared all legislative approval processes in all three countries and became effective as an international treaty on July 1, 2020. The general verdict is that Canada, through the work of a team of highly skilled negotiators, managed to contain its losses and preserve the essence of the original NAFTA. Significantly, the deal dropped the chapter on investor-state dispute settlement, which had served as the most prominent lightning rod for critics of the original deal. Such a chapter, ironically, was what Foreign Affairs Minister Chrystia Freeland had sought to "modernize" in the Canada-Chile free trade agreement.

∗ ∗ ∗

Although most of the world economy safely emerged from the 2008 – 2009 financial crisis, that sharp recession and its aftermath contributed to major shifts in public perceptions. Whereas the mainstream view of the globalized economy before the financial crisis was that "a rising tide lifts all boats," the recession exposed a shocking disparity between average incomes in many of the world's developed economies with a growing concentration of financial resources in the hands of the world's wealthiest. Perceptions of increasing inequality and income stagnation were factors in the success of Justin Trudeau's Liberals in the 2015 election, built on promises to strengthen the middle class and "those working hard to join it," as the slogan went. But in the United States politics took a less conventional turn, as they did in Britain where voters narrowly approved a referendum favouring Brexit, Britain's withdrawal from the European Union.

Well-founded perceptions of growing economic inequity worldwide made the pursuit of international trade agreements a much harder sell than a few years before. Those agreements were significantly to blame for rising inequality, in the views of many. This was fertile ground for the growth of protectionism and a rejection of the notion that steady and incremental opening of world markets leads on average to greater prosperity worldwide. To counter this, the government of Canada struggled to define a "progressive trade agenda" that aimed to convince Canadians that trade deals could be negotiated to foster better economic outcomes for Canadians. To date, there is little evidence that new measures so far negotiated in the European, Trans-Pacific or Chilean agreements on gender, labour, and environmental rights are anything more than hortatory.

∗ ∗ ∗

The streets of Moscow offered insight into income disparity in post-Cold War Russia when I participated in air traffic negotiations in the early 2000s. Only steps from Red Square were car dealerships selling Jaguars and Maseratis, not much farther away was a garishly illuminated casino. The excesses of Russia's fledgling market economy were provocations to many Russians for whom the promise of a freer society had not improved living standards. Rather, their lives were tainted by widespread economic misery. In the early 2000s, there was still hope though that Russia and the West could move closer together with more common understandings of civil freedoms and open markets. Former prime minister Jean Chrétien mused in his memoirs:

> The integration of Russia into the EU would have added a population of 175 million people and the vast resources of this immense country, the largest in the world, to the common European market . . . Europe would have gained even more power and influence . . .What possibilities for our Western world! . . . Imagine where we would be today if we had continued on the path of reconciliation with Russia.[1]

But a further plunge in living standards soured many Russians on the promise of free markets and encouraged Vladimir Putin to mobilize Russians around a new nationalism. The rapid expansion of NATO to former Warsaw Pact nations sowed distrust in Russian officialdom about Western intentions. The touted post-Cold War peace dividend that encouraged, for example, the MOX fuel disarmament initiative in which I took part, vanished like so many speculative mining shares. At the same time, Russia was trying to reclaim its post-Cold War influence, and among other questionable acts, finding in a corrupt South African President Jacob Zuma a willing buyer of its nuclear technology.

Global Affairs' commitment to economic growth through greater international trade was fundamental to its mission. So was the conviction held by many of my colleagues that human rights promotion would lead to a better world of more enlightened regimes, fostering economic opportunities, and civil freedoms. Trade and human rights would work in tandem. Free markets would produce more independent economic actors, who would themselves strive to create freer societies.

As I took leave of the department, that faith was being severely challenged. Rather than cultivating a more open and tolerant society, an increasingly powerful China, for example, was not only becoming more authoritarian in practice but was revising its ideology to justify it. "Xi Jinping Thought on Socialism with Chinese Characteristics for a New Era" eschewed discussion of human rights. Point five of the 14-point program states: "Improving people's livelihood and well-being is the primary goal of development." Of course. But in Xi Jinping thought, political freedoms are impediments to a harmoniously working society and greater prosperity, not tools to reach those goals. And China rewards regimes that share its disparaging views of political freedom.

I had seen the growing economic influence of China in my diplomatic postings. Chinese construction firms were active in Namibia, and their textile firms in South Africa supplying Chinese-origin labour not subject to those countries' labour codes. Chinese miners bought their way into the Madagascar mining sector with direct payments to the then-unelected government. The Zuma government in South Africa pursued a wholly uncritical course of closer relations with China through the BRICS and strongly supported the Shanghai-based New Development Bank, a BRICS initiative heavily relying on Chinese capital. At a Chinese-sponsored seminar in Santiago, Chile, I first heard of the "belt-and-road" initiative, China's plan to build a network of transportation infrastructure encircling the globe. As I left my assignment there, Chinese investors were beginning to make major plays in the resource sector, including by purchasing some Canadian-held assets.

Readers will have noticed that these memoirs did not address one of Canada's most significant foreign policy challenges in the era described here: our participation in the war on Afghanistan initially to oust the instigators of the 9/11 terrorist attack and to try to install an effectively secular democratic regime. It was my good fortune not to have been assigned to any posts directly involving that war. But striving to build a more stable and democratic Afghanistan was clearly a worthy – if eventually futile – challenge for Canadian foreign policy.

In today's world, old liberal verities are being supplanted by growing authoritarian ones. This is the broad tendency. But the big trends are often just background in the practical, day-to-day conduct of diplomacy, the plane on which most employees of foreign ministries function most of the time. In my own specific experience, those more practical tasks were, for instance, acquiring airline routes, managing softwood lumber quotas, handing out cultural grants, facilitating travel for foreign visitors, organizing attendance at international meetings, helping companies make foreign sales and investments, and other activities, some more tangible than others.

Practical exchanges among international friends and neighbours continue, often irrespective of ideology. In this more pedestrian world, a number of accomplishments stand out for me as highlights during my time working for Canada, promoting our interests abroad.

My participation in the embassy-led roundtables with Canadian mining firms in Santiago, Chile opened my eyes to the degree to which "corporate social responsibility" has become such an important part of companies' business planning. There is the realization that without the support of local communities and without abiding by the strictest environmental standards, companies will simply not be able to build their projects and achieve returns for shareholders. If there are still companies that exploit communities in some countries with poorly regulated resource planning, my experience in Chile demonstrated the value of CSR-oriented companies operating in concert with mining administrations that have an eye on sustainable development. This atmosphere proved critical to the Chilean government's adoption of a modified Canadian model for project approvals, which served both Chile's and Canada's interests and was a direct outcome of the Canadian embassy's efforts. (That our model seemed to work better in Chile than in our own country, given the uncertainty that still, for example, plagues the Trans Mountain Pipeline, says much about the constitutional tangle among our provinces, Indigenous communities and our courts).

The advocacy that led to a Canadian company's obtaining its licence to operate a multi-billion-dollar project in Madagascar, while at the same time encouraging a return to democracy in that island state, was a critical achievement for the Canadian high commission in South Africa. The tightly choreographed representation with like-minded embassies and international organizations such as La Francophonie was a model of how a country with Canada's reputation and diplomatic resources can achieve a result in Canadian interests.

A lot of international travel is as much a burden as a perquisite for diplomats. The destinations can be fascinating; the process of getting there and back in this security-conscious age can be aggravating. Nonetheless, when I consider the agreements negotiated with a range of countries during my air traffic negotiations team assignment, they expanded Canada's connections to foreign markets, big and small. The network of international air traffic rights, overseen by the International Civil Aviation Organization (ICAO), is a remarkable example of how international cooperation can provide a modern, safe and secure public good – largely free of political meddling and ideological bias – that benefits the entire global community.

The war in Kosovo in 1999 was a qualified success for the fledging "responsibility to protect" (R2P) doctrine. Albanian-speaking Kosovars were rescued from the kind of "ethnic cleansing" experienced earlier by the people of neighbouring Bosnia. Global Affairs' communications efforts at the time contributed to the Canadian public's general support for Canada's largest military intervention since the Korean War. Still, R2P is a contentious doctrine. Kosovo may have been one of its only successful applications. The 2011 war to back anti-Khadafy rebels in Libya, during which Canada sometimes justified its aerial bombardment under the R2P doctrine, opened an era of ongoing violence in Libya that has not subsided at the time of writing.

Some achievements during my time at Global Affairs were ambiguous. South Africa is an important political and commercial partner for Canada, but our relations had become fractious. If the Canadian high commission worked hard to improve the relationship during my assignment, it was difficult to determine if we were succeeding when I left in 2013. Certainly, that most prominent irritant, the *de jure* prohibition on travel to Canada by pre-1990 members of the African National Congress remained in place. The evident political will to remove the restriction never persuaded security officials to give up their resistance. Yet Canada's re-joining the countries that endorse the international convention on the prevention of climate change certainly brought Canada's and South Africa's policies into realignment in that area. And the replacement of President Zuma by President Cyril Ramaphosa, who wanted to root out the corruption of his predecessor, made the South African government a more palatable interlocutor.

My administrative role in the elimination of Promart, the international arts promotion program, evokes mixed feelings. It was perhaps my biggest management challenge, and I was pleased – putting aside my personal views of the importance of the arts in public diplomacy – with being able to wind it down without bureaucratic mishap and in a professional manner. Still, I came to see the program as a valuable one that could lift Canada's profile and burnish our identity abroad. I am unconvinced that the new resources put into cultural diplomacy by the current government are gaining the same traction.

Diplomacy is often seen as arcane and elitist. I hope that this memoir shows that it is neither. At its peak, the work of diplomacy is strenuous and focused on results. Even official cocktail parties, seen by some as trivial entertainments, and certainly rites carefully choreographed and frequently endured, do keep up diplomatic networks and gather intelligence. What I have tried to weave through this narrative is a portrait of the variety of activities that constitute diplomatic work.

Also, contrary to its elite reputation, the Department offers opportunities that Canadians from many economic and social strata have seized and mastered. Among heads of mission whom I served were the daughter of a hunting and camping outfitter, and the son of an immigrant steelworker. Another put himself through university picking cherries in the summer in the Okanagan, where he also learned English. I am the immigrant son of a father, who was an architectural draughtsman, and a mother, who was a peace activist, who encouraged my interest in international affairs. Growing up in a suburb of modest bungalows in southwest Calgary did not predestine me for a career in Canadian diplomacy.

Most officers in the Canadian foreign service pride themselves on their commitment to the work of diplomacy and they comprise collectively a group who believe they have been selected by merit. However, this cohesion has been undermined in recent years with the falling into disuse of the national foreign service competitions which used to be the point of access to a foreign service career. Those competitions used to take place annually, with senior departmental officials fanning out across the country to conduct interviews on university campuses. These boards would identify candidates for defined political, international trade, and consular "streams." In recent years, these contests have not been held, and many recruits have come from various university international affairs or MBA programs, hired individually on short-term contracts, and made permanent employees later. This has caused consternation among some of the past cohorts of the traditional competitions. It is their argument that the vocation of a diplomat who follows a formal career path and develops particular skills and specialties is being eroded. The absence of national competitions has the shortcoming of not recruiting regularly and systematically from all regions of Canada. I observed continuously during my tenure in the Department that my colleagues hailed from all parts of the country. It was always gratifying to me to meet officers originally from my home province of Alberta, and from Saskatchewan where I launched my journalistic career. That said, I wasn't recruited through any of those national competitions. My departmental career followed the earlier one in journalism, and to me, it was satisfying that the Department did recognize that it could benefit from expertise outside the traditional diplomatic, international trade, and consular "streams."

During the time in which I worked at Foreign/Global Affairs, the workforce has become increasingly diverse, such that the proportion of Department's employees who are women or who are visible minorities comes close to matching those proportions in the Canadian labour market at large.

Diplomacy is a conservative *métier* by nature. Foreign ministries exchange diplomatic notes. Ambassadors undertake démarches. Negotiated texts are sanctified in agreed minutes. These hoary means and procedures are used precisely because everyone, from no matter what kind of regime they hail, understands them. They are ways of stripping away the superfluous and communicating through a common language. Foreign ministries are usually mirrored images of themselves, with a few variations. They have bureaus of bilateral and multilateral affairs. They have geographic desks, legal bureaux and policy directorates, and, of course, offices of protocol. The traditional architecture of diplomatic work contributes to its longevity. Diplomacy will endure, largely using the same methods and structures as in the past, to avoid confusion and misunderstanding and provide a bulwark – although not an impregnable one it barely needs mentioning – for international stability.

The dryness of diplomacy's formal practices does not detract from the vitality of its purpose. I consider myself extremely fortunate to have entered this world when I was hired by the Department of External Affairs and International Trade in 1990. As a journalist, I was comfortable being a generalist. Once I had won the department's confidence, I was offered a wide variety of diverse assignments. My career was a continuing education. I conceived and organized communications strategies. I participated in trade negotiations. I administered trade controls. I managed cultural grants. I advocated for Canadian positions to heads of state. I promoted the interests of Canadian companies. And I learned to master some of the arts of management in a complex government bureaucracy. In all of this, there were few moments when I didn't believe I was serving Canadians, furthering our country's interests in a complex and multi-faceted international environment.

In my postings abroad, I had the great fortune to be accompanied by my wife, Suzanne. The role of the diplomatic spouse is often underappreciated. In so many cases, spouses offer unheralded support to their partners and the work of Canadian missions. The government of Canada provides allowances that compensate to a small degree for spouses' loss of employment opportunities when going abroad. But their knowledge and expertise often add considerable value to a diplomat's mission. In Suzanne's case, she established an exemplary network among other foreign missions in Pretoria to promote the French language; gave occasional administrative assistance to the missions; and deployed her considerable aptitude in the areas of hospitality and protocol during both ministerial and governor-general visits in both South Africa and Chile. Both I and the missions to which I was accredited benefited from her lifetime of knowledge, her unfailing charm, and her natural grace.

The world of 2019 is much different than that of 1989. As this book contends, we have passed through a distinct historical era, leaving behind the tense lands of the Cold War, traversing the high tide of liberal internationalism to reach the murky shores of a new, uncertain epoque yet to be named. For Canada, the foreign policy challenges of today's unanchored world are as great, or greater than, any we have encountered as a nation before. Dealing with them will be the responsibility of my ex-colleagues and the future recruits of Global Affairs Canada. What is clear is, that in working for Canada, there will be plenty of work to do.

Notes

NOTES TO PROLOGUE

1   From François-René de Chateaubriand, *Memoires d'outre-tombe* (Paris: Garnier, 1998), 1541, "Je me suis rencontré entre les deux siécles comme au confluent de deux fleuves. J'ai plongé dans leur eaux troublées, m'éloignant à regret du vieux rivage où j'étais né, et nageant avec espérance vers la rive inconnue . . ." English translation by the author.

2   William Wordsworth, "The Prelude," in *William Wordsworth*, ed. Stephen Gill (Oxford: Oxford University Press, 2010), 475.

3   Charles Taylor, *Hegel and Modern Society* (Cambridge: Cambridge University Press, 2015), 119.

NOTES TO CHAPTER 1

1   Leonard Cohen, "Democracy," in *The Future* (New York: Sony/ATV Music Publishing LLC, 1992).

2   Please see Prologue, xi.

3   Mulroney, Brian, *Memoirs* (Toronto: McClelland and Stewart, 2007), 829–30.

4   Daily Gulf reports, Government of Canada, National Archives (RG 25) Vol. 13184, File 57-12-8-1.

5   Daily Gulf reports.

6   Ann L. Hibbard and T.A. Keenleyside, "The Press and the Persian Gulf Crisis; The Canadian Angle," *Canadian Journal of Communication* 20, no.2 (1995): para. 5, https://doi.org/10.22230/cjc.1995v20n2a869.

7   Major Jean Morin and Lieutenant-Commander Richard H. Gimblett, *Operation Friction, The Canadian Forces in the Persian Gulf 1990–1991* (Toronto: Dundurn Press, 1997), 169–170. The officers were Captain Stephen Hill and Major David Kendall.

8   Daily Gulf Reports, op. cit. The report cites as its reference *The Globe and Mail*.

9   Canadian diplomat Michel Têtu. Of course, in 1991 President Bush did not pursue this line to its conclusion, eschewing the overthrow of Saddam Hussein after Kuwait's sovereignty had been secured. His son, George W. Bush did follow through 13 years later by waging the second Gulf War.

10   John Karlsrud, "For the greater good?: 'Good States' turning UN peacekeeping towards counter-terrorism," *International Journal: Canada's Journal of Global Policy Analysis* (March 19, 2019), https://doi.org/10.1177/00207020119834725.

NOTES TO CHAPTER 2

1   The provision ensuring that Canada supplies to the US market in times of shortage has never been invoked. In recent years, the Canadian petroleum industry has faced the opposite problem. Access has been impeded by US regulatory measures often imposed for environmental reasons. The assertion that the FTA just reflected the IEA agreement was more than debatable. It's a cooperative agreement among 17 member countries and provides for no enforcement provisions.

2   Michael Hart, Bill Dymond, and Colin Robertson, *Decision at Midnight: Inside the Canada-US Free Trade Negotiations* (Vancouver: UBC Press, 1994), 344.

3   Prominent members of the team were Frances Phillips, a former Financial Post reporter and a capable Spanish speaker after an assignment in Mexico; Trina Oviedo, a Venezuelan-Canadian still completing her undergraduate degree and later political first secretary in Canada's embassy to Congo; Rosemarie Boyle, an ex CBC journalist who would later become executive assistant to Bank of Canada Governor Stephen Poloz; and Jacqueline Bogden, a bright and enthusiastic officer also then completing her undergraduate degree. She subsequently became a senior executive in the Canadian public service, rising in recent years to assistant deputy minister at Health Canada where she oversaw the passage of legislation legalizing marijuana and headed a task force on the COVID-19 pandemic. Providing overall executive direction to our team was Christine Desloges, director of the Department's trade communications division and later Canada's ambassador to Vietnam. Paul Giroux, her deputy director, gave logistical support, and later left the government for more lucrative private sector opportunities.

4   Global Affairs Canada, *Foreign Trade – Treaties and Agreements – Free Trade Agreements – Canada-USA-Mexico – Third Party Relations* (37-3-4-2-4).

5   Global Affairs Canada, *Report of the Zacatecas negotiations, November 1991.*; Global Affairs Canada *Free Trade Agreements – Canada-USA-Mexico.*

6   External Affairs and International Trade Canada, *North American Free Trade Agreement: An Overview and Description*, 1992, identifier b2442516E, CA1 EA 92N51 ENG, accessed July 18, 2022, http://gac.canadiana.ca/view/ooe. b2442516E/170?r=0&s=1. The background package may be found at the above link, courtesy of the Global Affairs Canada library – a more polished package that included a trilaterally-agreed summary was released a week later.

7   The speech was given as part of the Ambassador Speaker Series hosted by the Norman Paterson School of International Affairs at Carleton University. It was delivered in the Senate Board Room of Robertson Hall.

NOTES TO CHAPTER 3

1   The Commission of Inquiry into the Sponsorship Program and Advertising Activities headed by retired judge John Gomery confirmed that funds set aside to raise awareness of federal programs in Quebec were diverted to the benefit of several Liberal Party operatives.

2   Question Period briefing note, BCD 0038.

3   "Gomery Phase One Report: Who is Responsible? Communication Agencies: Principals, Contracts and Interactions," *CBC*, November 1, 2005, 66, https://www.cbc.ca/news2/background/groupaction/gomeryreport_phaseone.html.

4   Lloyd Axworthy as cited by Andre Lui in *Why Canada Cares: Human Rights and Foreign Policy in Theory and Practice* (Montreal: McGill-Queen's University Press, 2012), 71.

5   See Bob Bergen, *Scattering Chaff: Canadian Air Power and Censorship during the Kosovo War* (Calgary: University of Calgary Press, 2019).

6   Pierre Martin and Michael Fortmaun, "Support for International Involvement in Canadian Public Opinion after the Cold War," *Canadian Military Journal* 2, no. 2, (2000), www.journal.forces.gc.ca/Vo2/No3.

7   Rumyana Vakarelska, "UK to steer plutonium processing projects by year end," *Reuters Events – Nuclear*, October 8, 2015, https://www.reutersevents.com/nuclear/waste-management/uk-steer-plutonium-processing-projects-year-end.

NOTES TO CHAPTER 4

1   Edward Shevardnadze, "Soviet Union's Foreign Policy," interview by Pravda, June 26, 1990, https://www.cvce.eu/en/obj/interview_with_edward_shevardnadze_on_the_soviet_union_s_foreign_policy_26_june_1990-en-680cef25-e267-420a-9bce-432704074e20.html.

2   Steven Lee Myers, "Suicide Bomber Kills 5 in Moscow Near Red Square," *New York Times*, December 10, 2003, https://www.nytimes.com/2003/12/10/world/suicide-bomber-kills-5-in-moscow-near-red-square.html.

3   J. Hartog, *Aruba: Short History* (Aruba: Van Dorp, 1988), 74.

4   Accorded the principal responsibility to conduct Canada's bilateral relations with a country without an embassy being on site.

5   Several government officials, including in ministerial offices, familiar with the meeting.

6   Karen Howlett, "No fly list ends beach vacation," *The Globe and Mail*, January 7, 2006, https://www.theglobeandmail.com/news/national/no-fly-list-ends-beach-vacation/article701111/.

NOTES TO CHAPTER 5

1   "Canadian Council Of Forest Ministers (CCFM): Preparing Forestry For The Next Century" *Canadian Intergovernmental Conference Secretariat*, September 20, 1999, https://scics.ca/en/product-produit/news-release-canadian-council-of-forest-ministers-ccfm-preparing-forestry-for-the-next-century/.

2   Elaine Feldman, "Some Lessons from the Last Softwood (Lumber IV) Dispute," *University of Calgary: The School of Public Policy Publications, Volume* 10, no 24, October 2017.

3   Feldman, "Some Lessons from the Last Softwood (Lumber IV) Dispute."

4   Charles Dickens, *Bleak House* (New York: Alfred A. Knopf, 1991), 95.

5   Katie Hoover and Ian F. Ferguson, *The 2006 US-Canada Softwood Lumber Agreement (SLA); In Brief,* Congressional Research Service, May 18, 2017, https://sgp.fas.org/crs/misc/R44851.pdf.

NOTES TO CHAPTER 6

1   Cited in John Hilliker, Mary Halloran, and Greg Donaghy, *Canada's Department of External Affairs, Volume III, Innovation and Adaptation 1968–1984* (Toronto: University of Toronto Press, 2017), 196.

2   Donald Savoie, *Whatever Happened to the Music Teacher? How Government Decides and Why* (Montreal: McGill-Queen's University Press, 2013), 148.

3   Savoie, *Whatever Happened to the Music Teacher?,* 138.

4   Savoie, *Whatever Happened to the Music Teacher?,* 150.

5   Cultureenperil, "Culture en péril (version longue)," September 23, 2008, https://www.youtube.com/watch?v=n3HVFsIQ5M4.

6   Paul Wells, *The Longer I'm Prime Minister: Stephen Harper and Canada, 2006* (Toronto: Random House Canada, 2013), 169.

NOTES TO CHAPTER 7

1   They had sought from within the ministry to project the view that the government was open to modifying the apartheid system. Jacobs had been in the South African embassy in Bonn in the late '80s when black and "coloured" rugby players were brought in to participate in international contests in Germany. Although scorned by many anti-apartheid activists, these contests were signs that the apartheid regime was starting to soften some of the most rigid attitudes (that blacks and whites could not play on the same field was one of apartheid many excesses).

2   "Factsheet: South Africa's crime statistics for 2016/17," *Africa Check,* October 24, 2017, https://africacheck.org/factsheets/south-africas-crime-statistics-201617.

3   Canada (Minister of Citizenship and Immigration) v. Huntley, (2010) 375 F.T.R. 250 (FC), para. 8.

4   Huntley, para. 9.

5   Huntley, para. 15.

6   Huntley, para. 57.

7   Huntley, para. 156.

8   Huntley, para. 254.

9   E-mail between Russell Kaplan and the author.

10   Refugee Appeal Division, Immigration and Refugee Board of Canada, 2016 CanLII 37544 (CA IRB); 2016-01-22; 6; Anonymous South African appellants in closed hearing seeking to overturn a negative ruling by the IRB, denying claims of persecution on the basis of race and political opinion.

11   E-mail interview with the author, April 6, 2018.

NOTES TO CHAPTER 8

1 Promit Mukherjee, "Arms deal corruption trial against South African ex-President Zuma to start in May," *Thomson Reuters*, February 23, 2021, https://www.reuters.com/article/us-safrica-zuma-idUSKBN2AN0W2.

2 Marianne Thamm, "Khwezi, the woman who accused Jacob Zuma of rape, dies," *The Guardian*, October 10, 2016, https://www.theguardian.com/world/2016/oct/10/khwezi-woman-accused-jacob-zuma-south-african-president-aids-activist-fezekile-ntsukela-kuzwayo.

3 BBC, "South African President Jacob Zuma 'is a sex addict,'" *Modern Ghana*, February 2, 2010, https://www.modernghana.com/news/261780/south-africa-president-jacob-zuma-is-a-sex-addict.html.

4 Stephen Chan, *Old Treacheries, New Deceits: Insights into Southern African Politics* (Cape Town: Jonathan Bell Publishers, 2011), 250.

5 Mike De Souza, "Canada's anti-Kyoto stance sours climate-change discussions in Durban," *Nunatsiaq News*, July 20, 2022, https://nunatsiaq.com/stories/article/65674canadas_anti-kyoto_stance_sours_climate_change_discussions_in_durban/.

NOTES TO CHAPTER 9

1 Daron Acemoglu and James A. Robinson, *Why Nations Fail: The Origins of Power, Prosperity, and Poverty* (New York: Crown Publishing Group, 2012).

2 Fred Khumalo, "Zuma's Song," *Sunday Times*, December 23, 2012, https://www.timeslive.co.za/sunday-times/lifestyle/2012-12-23-zumas-song/. Not knowing isiZulu, I compared my notes with this *Sunday Times* account of the conference.

3 These words are paraphrased from Nelson Mandela's famous autobiography *Long Walk to Freedom* (New York: Little Brown & Co., 1994).

4 That Mandela was suffering from dementia was confirmed to me by a diplomatic source who was particularly well-connected to the Mandela family.

5 Nick Thompson and Kim Norgaard, "Video of ailing Nelson Mandela prompts outrage in South Africa," *CNN*, May 2, 2013, https://www.cnn.com/2013/04/30/world/africa/south-africa-mandela-video/index.html

6 Erin Conway-Smith, "The curious case of the death of Malawi's president," *GlobalPost*, March 20, 2013, https://theworld.org/stories/2013-03-20/curious-case-death-malawi-s-president. Malawi President Bingu wa Mutharika died suddenly in April 2012. To delay the appointment to the presidency of vice-president Joyce Banda, the president's brother, who had ambitions to replace him, claimed he was still alive. In a rather elaborate ruse, the corpse – with medical equipment attached – was flown to a South African military base to be transported to a Pretoria hospital where he would supposedly receive treatment unavailable in Malawi. Although the South African pilot initially refused to transport the obviously lifeless body, the plane took off after the South African high commissioner was summoned to the airport by Malawian authorities. But after their arrival in South Africa, President Jacob Zuma refused to go along with the charade and announced Mutharika's death two days after the fact. Despite Zuma's role in lifting the shroud of mystery in the Malawi case, many South

Africans – highly skeptical of Zuma and many of his ANC comrades – promoted the notion South African authorities were concocting their own Malawi caper.

7   President Cyril Ramaphosa acknowledged to the Zondo Commission's Inquiry into Allegations of State Capture, Corruption and Fraud in the Public Sector Including Organs of State that state procedures regarding the Russian nuclear deal were not followed by Jacob Zuma, his predecessor. "Commission of Inquiry into State Capture," Part II, Volume 6, sections 235 and 244, pages 98 and 102, accessed July 18, 2022, www.statecapture.org.za.

8   The Zondo Commission "establish(ed) that . . . the extensive scheme of corruption and wrongdoing that afflicted public entities, government departments and other state agencies of South Africa (were present) during the period under review, notably, but not exclusively, at the instances of the Gupta enterprise." "Commission of Inquiry into State Capture," Part II, Vol. 6, sections 69 and 70, pages 32 and 33.

9   A detailed account of the corrupt tender process for Transet's rail equipment is contained in the Zondo Commissions's inquiry, "Commission of Inquiry into State Capture," Part II, Volume 1: Transnet, 1–494.

NOTES TO CHAPTER 10

1   The Economist, *Pocket World in Figures, 2018 Edition* (New York: The Economist Newspaper Ltd., 2017).

2   In the interest of privacy and to protect the identities of those involved, neither names nor specific details of these cases are divulged here.

3   As translated from French in my notes.

4   Although certainly the largest, Sherritt's Ambatovy mine and refinery were not the only facilities in Madagascar with Canadian links. On the far southern tip of Madagascar at Fort Dauphin is QMM. Originally standing for Quebec Madagascar Mines and Minerals, the ilmenite mine was acquired by the British-Australian company, Rio Tinto, but some of its personnel continued to be Canadian. The ore, a combination of titanium and iron, comes from a surface deposit that is essentially scraped away and milled before being shipped to a refinery in Sorel, Quebec. QMM was also being caught by the regime's efforts to generate more revenues.

5   In the subsequent election, archrivals Rajoelina and Ravalomanana finally confronted each other at the polls. Rajoelina emerged the victor, his transformation from militarily installed consul to elected president at last complete.

NOTES TO CHAPTER 11

1   "Senador Quintana anuncia 'retroexcavadora' contra modelo neoliberal," *Emol Nacional*, March 25, 2014, https://www.emol.com/noticias/nacional/2014/03/25/651676/nueva-mayoria-advierte-que-pasara-retroexcavadora.html.

2   In fact, this perspective was promoted by one of the advisors of Pinochet who sought to give his rule legitimacy. Jaime Guzmán was founder of Chile's most right-wing political party, the Unión Demócrata Independiente (UDI). Guzmán was gunned down in an act of unalloyed political revenge by leftist assassins in the early days of the restored democracy.

3   "Empresarios le dicen a Bachelet en su cara que las reformas son el origen de la incertidumbre económica," *El Mostrador,* November 6, 2014, https://www.elmostrador.cl/noticias/pais/2014/11/06/sofofa-cuestiona-reformas-del-gobierno-y-las-severas-criticas-al-rol-del-sector-privado/.

4   "Corte Suprema paraliza proyecto minero El Morro de Goldcorp," *La Tercera,* October 7, 2014, https://www.latercera.com/noticia/corte-suprema-paraliza-proyecto-minero-el-morro-de-goldcorp/.

NOTE TO EPILOGUE

1   Jean Chrétien, *My Stories, My Times* (New York: Penguin Random House, 2018), 59–60.

CPSIA information can be obtained
at www.ICGtesting.com
Printed in the USA
BVHW031527231022
649852BV00004B/19